SAVE MORE TOMORROW

SAVE MORE TOMORROW

PRACTICAL BEHAVIORAL FINANCE
SOLUTIONS TO IMPROVE 401(K) PLANS

SHLOMO BENARTZI
WITH ROGER LEWIN

PORTFOLIO / PENGUIN

PORTFOLIO / PENGUIN
Published by the Penguin Group
Penguin Group (USA) Inc., 375 Hudson Street,
New York, New York 10014, U.S.A.
Penguin Group (Canada), 90 Eglinton Avenue East, Suite 700,
Toronto, Ontario, Canada M4P 2Y3
(a division of Pearson Penguin Canada Inc.)
Penguin Books Ltd, 80 Strand, London WC2R 0RL, England
Penguin Ireland, 25 St. Stephen's Green, Dublin 2, Ireland
(a division of Penguin Books Ltd)
Penguin Books Australia Ltd, 250 Camberwell Road, Camberwell,
Victoria 3124, Australia
(a division of Pearson Australia Group Pty Ltd)
Penguin Books India Pvt Ltd, 11 Community Centre, Panchsheel Park,
New Delhi—110 017, India
Penguin Group (NZ), 67 Apollo Drive, Rosedale, Auckland 0632,
New Zealand (a division of Pearson New Zealand Ltd)
Penguin Books (South Africa) (Pty) Ltd, 24 Sturdee Avenue,
Rosebank, Johannesburg 2196, South Africa

Penguin Books Ltd, Registered Offices:
80 Strand, London WC2R 0RL, England

First published in 2012 by Portfolio / Penguin,
a member of Penguin Group (USA) Inc.

10 9 8 7 6 5 4 3

Authors' Note
The authors believe the principles and strategies suggested by this book will significantly improve retirement outcomes for workers and improve the effectiveness of employers' employee benefits programs. However, the authors are behavioral economists, not lawyers, and we do not intend this book to address the full spectrum of the various legal requirements associated with plan design and administration. We therefore urge plan sponsors and plan fiduciaries to consult legal counsel and other appropriate expert advice prior to making changes to their plans.

Library of Congress Cataloging-in-Publication Data

Benartzi, Shlomo.
Save more tomorrow : practical behavioral finance solutions to improve 401(k) plans / Shlomo Benartzi with Roger Lewin.
p. cm.
Includes bibliographical references and index.
ISBN 978-1-59184-484-6
1. Finance, Personal—Psychological aspects. 2. Pension trusts—Investments. 3. Individual retirement accounts. I. Lewin, Roger. II. Title.
HG179.B386 2012
332.024'0145—dc23
2011052895
Printed in the United States of America
Set in Janson Text
Designed by Pauline Neuwirth

ACKNOWLEDGMENTS

This book is a central part of the PlanSuccess System, a system dedicated to providing behavioral solutions to improve 401(k) plans. PlanSuccess is the first major initiative of the Allianz Global Investors Center for Behavioral Finance. The Center is dedicated to improving financial outcomes for people by helping them make better financial decisions, and I am delighted to be working with Allianz Global Investors toward that objective. Thank you to those who have actively contributed to or supported this work: Cathy Smith, Horacio Valeiras, Marna Whittington, Brian Gaffney, Glenn Dial, Andy Wilmot, and Bruce Wolfe. I would also like to thank the members of the Center's academic advisory board for their contributions that helped bring this book into being. They include: Nicholas Barberis, Kent Daniel, Dan Goldstein, and Noah J. Goldstein.

Special thanks are due to Jamie Hayes, an outstanding financial adviser whose grounded advice helped make this book useful and practical; and to John Payne, who worked very closely with me and Roger and was always a reliable source of novel and pertinent perspectives. And very special thanks to Richard Thaler. Richard is the other intellectual "parent" of the highly successful savings-enhancement program, Save More Tomorrow™, which, of course, is the inspiration for the title of this book. I have been truly blessed working with him on our Save More Tomorrow™ program, and on other ventures in behavioral finance, for the last two decades. John and Richard are both members of the Center's academic advisory board as well.

I would also like to acknowledge the help of the following people, listed alphabetically: James Choi, Hal Hershfield, Sheena Iyengar, Charles Kreitler, Brigitte Madrian, Gergana Nenkov, Alessandro Previtero, and Steve Shu; the research support of Anna Wroblewska; and the organizing skills of Caitlin Ledwith and Kim Andranovich.

And close to my heart are Shalom, my dad, who taught me so much, and Leah, my mom. A deeply felt thank-you to you both. I'd like also to thank Lesli, my wife, and Maya, our little girl, for joining me on this fun journey of writing a book.

When I sat down to compose these acknowledgments I intended to limit my major thanks to just seven people, because I love the number seven. (We'll learn more about "the magic number seven" and its implications for investment choices in chapter seven.) I very quickly realized, as you will have noticed, that my gratitude extended far beyond that magic number. Well, I guess it is just the human element creeping in, and that's appropriate because this book is actually all about the human element and how it creeps in and influences people's decisions around 401(k) plans.

CONTENTS

SAVE MORE TOMORROW

INTRODUCTION

THE 401(K) WORLD IN CRISIS

During the past three decades, a major shift has been taking place in retirement systems in the United States and in the rest of the industrialized world. Traditional pensions that guaranteed lifelong income after retirement (based on years of service and salary prior to retirement) are being replaced with defined contribution retirement savings vehicles, the most common of which in the United States are known as 401(k)* plans. Defined contribution plans have been in existence for decades, of course, in various forms. But 401(k) plans have eventually come to play a very different role from the one originally intended for them.

When they were created by the Revenue Act of 1978, 401(k) plans were designed merely as a vehicle to supplement traditional pension plans: a little extra on the side, so to speak. But for a variety of economic and regulatory reasons, 401(k) plans began to replace traditional pension plans as the primary retirement savings vehicle for many people, slowly at first and then with increasing pace in the very recent past. The transition has been so sweeping that these "new" savings vehicles are rapidly coming to dominate the retirement savings landscape (Potbera et al., 2007).

As of 2005, of those private sector workers with pension coverage, 63 percent relied exclusively on 401(k) or similar defined contribution plans; 10 percent had only a defined benefit plan; and 27 percent had a combination of the two types of plan. Two decades earlier the distribution was one-third in each category

---

* This book is about the universe of defined contribution plans, that is, 401(k), 403(b), and 457 plans, even though we often refer to the entire universe of defined contribution plans as 401(k) plans.

(Employee Research Benefit Institute, 2007). In the realm of financial preparation for retirement, we are now essentially in a 401(k) world.

Employers like the shift, because with traditional defined benefit plans the financial burden of funding pensions and the risk associated with constructing and managing investment portfolios fell on them. Under 401(k) plans, by contrast, it is employees who assume most of that financial burden and all of that risk. Employees must not only fund their retirement accounts, whereas previously they did not, but they are also responsible for savings and investment decisions. Despite these new burdens, employees, too, might find 401(k) plans appealing, for several reasons.

First, unlike traditional pensions, 401(k) plans are readily portable between different employers. Employees, therefore, don't face the prospect of losing plan benefits when they switch employers. This is especially appealing to women, who, on average, go in and out of the workforce more frequently, often for reasons of family responsibilities.

Second, as mentioned, unlike traditional pensions, 401(k) plans give employees control over their retirement funds. They can choose whether or not they want to have an account. If they do elect to participate, they can decide how much to save, and how the funds will be invested. If they don't like taking risks, they can develop a very conservative portfolio. Bolder employees can, if they so wish, choose a more aggressive mix of assets. The freedom and responsibility offered by 401(k) plans make them potentially attractive to employees. But with freedom and responsibility come new opportunities and new challenges, too.

As noted above, in their initial formulation, 401(k) plans were designed to be supplementary savings accounts to employees' primary pension funds. In order to participate in these new savings accounts, employees had to take active steps to enroll, or opt in. The default setting for 401(k) plans, therefore, was non-participation; employees had to take action if they wanted to participate. This made sense, given that the plans were simply there to gather a little extra on the side—a piggy bank for "frivolous" expenditures, perhaps. The investment options offered through these new plans were initially extremely simple, often a single fixed-income fund, for example, or at most two—a stock fund and a fixed income fund. For instance, when the Teachers Insurance and Annuity Association (TIAA) formed the College Retirement Equities Fund (CREF) in 1952, participants were offered two investment options, a fixed-income fund and an equity fund. Prior to that date, and since it was founded in 1918, TIAA had offered only a fixed annuity. The number of menu options offered by TIAA-CREF in 2011 is forty-seven (Company Web site).

During the 401(k)'s evolution to becoming the primary savings vehicle for most workers' retirement, two things changed, and one did not. Important consequences have followed the new formulation:

▶ Now that 401(k) plans are most people's primary source of retirement income and not just offering a little extra on the side, the balance required when the account matures is vastly greater than it ever was.

▶ The savings and, especially, the investment options have become much more complex. For instance, in 2010 the average number of investment options in 401(k) plans was eighteen, up from one or two when defined contribution plans were first introduced, and doubled from a decade ago (PSCA, 2011).

▶ The default, opt-in status has remained unchanged, which, it could be argued, is no longer appropriate, given 401(k) plans' new role as the primary retirement savings account for most people who have retirement plans.

The increased complexity of 401(k) plans, combined with the continued requirement to actively opt in to become a participant, has presented employees with decision-making challenges they had not faced previously. The decision to opt in is just the first in an array of behavioral challenges employees face in this new retirement planning environment. Others include how much to save and, then, how to invest their assets. Many people find this increased complexity of retirement plan decision making overwhelming, and having a large menu of investment options from which to choose can be confusing. As a result, employees often make poor decisions and find themselves not doing "the right thing" for their retirement future.

In theory, workers should prosper under 401(k) plans. The reality, however, has turned out to be very different. For a start, almost 50 percent of private-sector workers (mostly in small companies) do not have access to 401(k) plans at all, often because their employers believe them to be too complex, difficult, and costly to administer. (This is not a failure of employees, of course, but more a failure of the system.) Of those who are eligible to participate, many are slow to enroll, and almost one-third fail entirely to do so, forgoing tax benefits and matching contributions from employers, as well as facing retirement years with only Social Security to support them.

Deciding to join a plan is, of course, the right thing to do, because when asked, most workers say they would like to save for retirement. Of those who do enroll, 39 percent don't save enough to receive the full employer match, and most fail to save enough to maintain their lifestyle after retirement. The average savings rate is around 6 percent, for instance, which is just over half the 10 percent recommended by most financial professionals. (When asked, most employees—68 percent—acknowledge that they aren't saving enough [Choi et al., 2006].) Young and lower-paid employees disproportionately fall behind in these measures.

In the realm of investment, plan participants typically do a rather poor job of managing their portfolios. Here's just one example. Warren Buffett once famously said, "Investors should remember that excitement and expenses are their enemies. And if they insist on trying to time their participation in equities, they should try to be fearful when others are greedy and greedy only when others are fearful."* Unfortunately, most individual investors do the opposite, and chase "hot" stocks, only to discover that what is hot one day can quickly turn cold the next. This was only too evident in the run-up of the stock market through the 1990s, when individual investors were enthusiastically pouring their retirement funds into equities, especially in the technology area. A lot of retirement accounts lost a lot of money in the market's subsequent precipitous decline. As I noted in a paper with Richard Thaler, the timing of these individual investors' exposure to the market was exactly wrong: "They bought high and sold low" (Benartzi and Thaler, 2007).

In other words, the great majority of people who participate in 401(k) plans don't save enough, and do a poor job of investing.

This latter fact is not surprising. After all, most people are not financial professionals (nor should they be expected to be) and are not well-versed in the workings of the world of finance. For instance, according to a 2002 survey by John Hancock Financial Services, 92 percent of people are unable to explain what a money market fund is (Hancock, 2002).

---

*   Chairman's letter to Berkshire Hathaway shareholders, 2004.

Summary of shortcomings of 401(k) plans:

- Half of all private-sector workers have no access to 401(k) plans
- Of those who do, almost one-third do not participate
- Most participants do not save enough
- Most participants do a poor job with investment decisions

The result of these various failures is that the future for most people who are approaching retirement is less than encouraging. According to Financial Engines' 2011 Survey of 401(k) Plans, almost three-quarters (72 percent) of Americans are not on track to reach retirement income goals by the time they are sixty-five. It is no surprise, then, that barely 13 percent of workers feel confident that they will have saved enough money to maintain their lifestyle after retirement, and that 74 percent expect to have to work after their retirement to supplement inadequate savings.[*]

In short, the 401(k) world is in crisis.

BEHAVIORAL CHALLENGES OF THE 401(K) WORLD

Imagine the following. You are at a cocktail party, and you meet Harry Markowitz, distinguished professor of finance at the University of California, and recipient of the Nobel Memorial Prize in Economic Sciences for his pioneering work on portfolio theory. You overcome your shyness and tentatively engage him in conversation about the challenges of managing portfolios. You are deeply impressed by his tremendous grasp of this complex subject, as of course you should be.

---

[*] Data from the 2011 Retirement Confidence Survey of the Employee Benefit Research Institute.

Question: Given what you knew about Professor Markowitz's towering intellect, his experience with portfolio theory, and your impression of him at the party, you would expect that he, more than the rest of us mere mortals, would have carefully analyzed his investment options when enrolling in his retirement savings plan, looking for the optimal trade-off between risk and return and the like. Correct?

Answer: Correct. But you would be wrong.

Here is what Markowitz told a writer for *Money* magazine about his decision to choose a 50/50 split between the one stock fund and the one bond fund that he was offered by the plan provider, TIAA-CREF, in the mid-1980s: "I visualized my grief if the stock market went way up and I wasn't in it—or if it went down and I was completely in it. My intention was to minimize my future regret" (Zweig, 1998).

"Minimize my future regret"? So much for the steel-trap analytical mind that economic theory expects us humans to apply to such decisions, and from the economics Nobel laureate in the topic at hand, no less. The decision Markowitz faced was not especially complex—just two investment options—and yet, instead of figuring out the optimal balance between the two, he felt compelled to fall back on a simple rule: divide the assets equally between them. (People often adopt this so-called 1/n rule of thumb when faced with uncertainty about how to allocate assets over a menu of funds [Benartzi and Thaler, 2001.]) To be fair to Markowitz, more than half of the participants in this same plan, many of whom were university professors of some stripe or other, also opted for a 50/50 split. Nor was Markowitz the only financial maven quoted in the *Money* magazine article to follow his gut feeling and simple rules rather than cool analysis in such retirement plan decisions.

The point of this story is that in the realm of decision making about 401(k) plans (as with much of human decision making, actually), we run squarely into the human element—the human factor, if you like. We enter the "behavioral world," where people sometimes make poor decisions, decisions that economists' much-touted "rational man" would never make. In Markowitz's case, his initial impulse was driven by his "intuitive mind," specifically in this case, the desire to avoid regret. His "reflective mind" then comes into play, but instead of using all the information he had at hand, Markowitz adopted the simple mental rule of thumb, or heuristic, we just described: dividing the assets equally between the available funds.

Markowitz's desire to minimize his future regret if he were to see his account balance go down is an example of what psychologists call "loss aversion," a very powerful and common psychological factor in human decision making. Loss aversion implies that losses loom in our minds about twice as large as equivalent gains. Indeed, loss aversion is one of the most powerful psychological factors at work in the field of behavioral economics and behavioral finance (Benartzi, 2011). (You will see this played out in Chapters 2, 5, and 8 in relation to enrolling, saving, and investing in 401(k) plans.) There are, however, many more psychological factors at work as well (Kahneman, 2003).

In the context of behavioral finance, as applied to decisions around 401(k) plans, we have identified the three psychological factors that we regard as most relevant. They are:

- **Loss aversion**—*the strong negative response to loss (described above)*
- **Inertia**—*the preference for the status quo*
- **Myopia**—*a detrimental focus on the short term*

These three factors are as simple as they are powerful. They underlie the important mistakes people make in the realms of the decision to enroll, how much to save, and how to invest, and they constitute the psychological backbone of *Save More Tomorrow*. You will come to see these three factors at work in some detail in the following chapters, but here is just a taste of the behavioral world you are entering as you read this book.

Inertia: Like loss aversion, inertia is a powerful force in human psychology. Most of us dislike change and cling to the familiar—the status quo. And we especially dislike change if it involves physical or mental effort. How many of us have vowed, either publicly or privately, at one time or other to start that new diet or sign up for that new exercise program? Most of us, I know. And we honestly say to ourselves, "I'll do it tomorrow." But as we know only too well, tomorrow all too often doesn't come, and we continue on the same old track. Procrastination ultimately leads to inaction.

In the realm of mistakes people make around 401(k) plan participation, inertia is the principal reason why one-third of eligible workers end up not enrolling, and hence not saving, for their retirement. Many workers become overwhelmed by the saving and investment decisions that go along with the process of enrolling in a plan. As a result, they say, "I'll figure all that out tomorrow." These are the same people who, when asked, will say they really would like to save for their retirement, if only they could get around to it.

Even when armed with information and good intentions, the behavioral challenges surrounding enrolling are insurmountable for many people. For instance, one study of the impact of an employer-provided financial education program found that 100 percent of the employees asserted that they now planned to enroll in the company's retirement plan as a result of what they had learned. After an average of three months later, only 14 percent of those people had acted on their good intentions (Choi et al., 2006).

Myopia: People have a strong tendency to focus inordinately on the immediate present, and cannot readily bring into mental focus the distant future—which makes us all Mr. Magoos where thinking about retirement is concerned. Mr. Magoo was an extremely nearsighted cartoon character who made his television debut in the U.S. in the 1960s. Those familiar with Mr. Magoo's antics on the screen know they typically led to hilarious, if often physically bruising, outcomes, as he shortsightedly blundered through life. Being myopic in the context of saving for retirement can, however, lead to more serious consequences, as we blunder into decisions that are detrimental to our future financial well-being.

For all but those on the threshold of retirement, thinking about that distant prospect is very difficult, and even more difficult to act upon, especially when action requires sacrifices in the present. Seduced by temporal myopia in their younger years, many people get around to saving seriously for their retirement far too late in their career, in their forties and fifties in many cases, which greatly reduces the amount of money they will have available for their retirement.

Even those workers who do the right thing and enroll in a retirement plan can be adversely affected by a different form of myopia, in the context of investment. Managing an investment portfolio over a period of three or more decades calls for long-range vision and a tolerance for the inevitable short-term fluctuations in the markets. Too many people obsess over short-term changes, however, and react negatively to short-term losses. These people succumb to what Richard Thaler and I call "myopic loss aversion." As a result, these investors adopt a very conservative investment strategy that diminishes their long-term returns. When investors instead consider long-term returns, they are willing to make more aggressive decisions, which are likely to benefit their ultimate wealth accumulation (Benartzi and Thaler, 1999).

For many young people, the choices around a retirement plan—whether to join, how much to save, and how to invest—represent the first major financial decisions of their lives, and perhaps the biggest ones they will ever make. Remarkably, most people, when newly hired, spend less than an hour pondering this momentous step (Benartzi and Thaler, 1999). Given the behavioral challenges that swirl around these decisions, it is not surprising that people sometimes make poor choices.

What can employers and their advisers do to help?

BEHAVIORAL FINANCE TOOLS CAN IMPROVE OUTCOMES

Embarking on a retirement savings program is akin to setting out on a long journey that presents varied and daunting challenges along the way. The power of this book is that the relatively new science of behavioral finance offers a novel way of addressing these challenges. Behavioral finance is an offshoot of behavioral economics, which is a combination of psychological principles and economic theory. Daniel Kahneman, a psychologist, was awarded the Nobel Prize in economics in 2002 for his seminal work on behavioral economics. Part of Kahneman's insight was his recognition of the important role of emotion and intuition in people's decision making that in certain circumstances leads to systematic and predictable errors, which is what we are calling behavioral challenges (Kahneman, 2003). Armed with these original scientific insights, we are able to guide people toward better decisions in the realm of retirement savings.

The thrust of this scientific approach is that the various *behavioral challenges* in this realm present opportunities for *novel behavioral solutions*. As a result, the journey to retirement can go smoothly and end as one would wish—that is, with sufficient funds to support a comfortable and dignified retirement. The key ingredient to successful behavioral tools is *making it easy* for people to overcome these challenges and achieve outcomes they say they want and are in their best interests. The behavioral finance toolbox we present in this book is a collection of seemingly simple, but powerful, actions. These actions help people make the kinds of decisions they might reach if, empowered with the right information, they sat down and carefully thought about the challenges they face.

As with every new science, some areas of the landscape are as yet more developed than others. This will change as time passes and more research is done. At the same time, some behavioral solutions are, by their nature, more immediate and powerful than others. Shifting the architecture of a default from opt-in to opt-out, is an example of a simple but extremely powerful behavioral solution, as we will see with plan participation in Chapter 1. Other behavioral interventions are more cutting-edge and still need to be fine-tuned, such as engaging people's emotions and imaginations to enable them to see their future selves and their future lifestyles, as we will see in Chapters 3 and 6. Behavioral finance therefore arms us with behavioral solutions of different potencies. Whether you choose "bulletproof" behavioral solutions or newer cutting-edge ideas, you are gaining a practical edge in the goal of improving retirement planning.

By way of illustrating that this is a proven approach, here is one example that has made a tremendous impact on people's retirement savings behavior.

I chose *Save More Tomorrow* as the title for this book because it accurately describes much of my research. My mission is to apply the new science of behavioral finance to help people enjoy a comfortable retirement by helping them save more for tomorrow. But the title was also inspired by a savings enhancement program that my colleague Richard Thaler and I developed a decade ago, also called Save More Tomorrow™ (SMarT). SMarT is widely regarded as one of the most effective behavioral tools

ever developed (Kahneman, 2011). The program incorporates a
scientific understanding of people's behaviors around inertia,
loss aversion, and myopia. You will find a detailed description of
the program in Chapters 4 and 5. Suffice it to say here that the
program makes it easy for employees to start saving and to gradually increase their savings rate over a period of years—a decision that many people often find difficult to act on. The
improved outcome was impressive: it almost quadrupled retirement contributions (from 3.5 to 13.6 percent of income) among
employees at a mid-sized manufacturing company in the first
three and a half years of its initial implementation (Thaler and
Benartzi, 2004). The program is now used by more than half of
the large employers in the United States, and a variant of the
program was incorporated into the Pension Protection Act of
2006.

If all the behavioral challenges around executing a smart
401(k) plan, from enrolling, through accumulation, to decumulation, were as easily solved as was the case with SMarT (that is,
initiating and increasing savings), we would be able to end the
401(k) crisis tomorrow. Unfortunately, that is not quite the case.
There is, however, good reason for optimism, because the
behavioral interventions in the behavioral finance toolbox presented in the following chapters are smart enough to take us a
long way toward that desired goal.

Behavioral Architecture Guides the Way Forward

Brian Wansink, director of the Cornell University Food and
Brand Laboratory, has made something of a name for himself
figuring out what prompts people to eat under different circumstances. In his book *Mindless Eating* Wansink tells us to forget
fancy, expensive diets that require you to exert self-control if you
want to lose weight; they mostly don't work. Instead, he sug-

gests, make sure that when you open your refrigerator, the first things you see are morsels that are good for you, such as cherry tomatoes, sticks of celery, and the like. Keep that fudge sundae and other tempting but bad-for-you treats out of sight at the back of the shelf. Changing choices in your snacking environment, rather than hoping that willpower will work, is more likely to change what you end up snacking on, he says. And if you want to avoid the temptation of seconds at dinner, put that half-full dish of shepherd's pie in the kitchen, not within easy reach at the table. Such small changes in the eating environment can dramatically alter people's eating habits, says Wansink. He has done hundreds of experiments that prove his point.

Choice Architecture: These are some simple, homey examples of what Richard Thaler and Cass Sunstein* call "choice architecture" in their book, *Nudge: Improving Decisions About Health, Wealth, and Happiness.* Although the rest of their book is not about food, Thaler and Sunstein open it by describing the potential impact on the food choices of schoolchildren in a cafeteria: display food so that children see the salads before they get to the burgers, and they will eat more salad and fewer burgers. Simple. And powerful.

The point about these stories is that adults, like schoolchildren, are exquisitely sensitive to changes in the context in which they make choices. You think it best if people eat more salad? Put the salad front and center. You want to avoid the temptation of that oh-so-bad-for-you fudge sundae? Put it out of sight. Making the right choice then becomes much easier.

When people embark on the journey that is represented by their retirement savings program, they face choices every step

---

* Sunstein, who should know better, is also one of those TIAA-CREF participants who, like Markowitz, chose a 50/50 split, and didn't rebalance his portfolio for decades.

of the way. Many of the behavioral interventions in the behavioral finance toolbox focus on choice architecture. The goal is to make it easy for people to make those choices and, more importantly, to make the *right* choices. Here's one example—by now a familiar issue.

Financial advisers and plan sponsors know better than anyone that workers enjoy a more comfortable retirement if they enroll in a sound retirement savings plan early in their working lives. And, as we've said more than once, people readily admit they would like to do just that. So why do one out of three people who should enroll when they have the opportunity, fail to do so? Because, as we saw earlier, they must make an active decision to enroll, and at the very same time they must decide how much they will save and how they want to invest their assets. The complexities of these saving and investment decisions overwhelm many people, inertia takes grip, they do nothing, and by default they are left on the sidelines and not saving for their retirement.

The behavioral solution is simple. Change the choice architecture so that workers are automatically enrolled in the plan, with the freedom of opting out at any point they may wish. You will see in detail in Chapter 1 that the impact on plan participation of this simple switch in choice architecture is tremendous: it rises from 70 percent to more than 90 percent. The behavioral challenge was inertia in the face of complex decisions. The behavioral solution was to remove this complexity by implementing automatic enrollment. The decision that workers face under this new choice architecture is now very easy: whether to stay enrolled or to opt out. Most do nothing, and are on their journey toward accumulating sufficient money for their retirement.

Information Architecture: Choice architecture, then, is one aspect of the behavioral interventions we describe in the following chapters, and it is a very important one. People who are responsible for deciding how a choice is to be offered, such as plan sponsors selecting a particular default option for a 401(k) plan, are acting as choice architects. The second aspect of behavioral interventions, which we call information architecture, concerns how information is presented to people so that it is immediately comprehensible and engaging. People who are responsible for how information is conveyed are, of course, information architects.

Here's a cautionary tale, again involving food, which leads us into the realm of information architecture. In 2006, the New York City Department of Health passed legislation mandating that fast-food restaurants, among others, post calorie information on their menu boards. It seemed like a very good idea, given the current epidemic of obesity, especially among the young. The initiative was based on a simple notion: if people know that the meal they are planning to eat contains a lot of calories, they will do the sensible thing and cut back on what they consume. Researchers at Carnegie Mellon University were happy to take advantage of this natural experiment to test the efficacy of the information initiative. They surveyed patrons' food consumption at three fast-food outlets, before and after the legislation went into effect. The burghers of the New York City Council cannot have been too happy with the results.

Not only did the apparently sensible information campaign not have the desired effect—people did *not* hold back from ordering those big burgers—it actually had what the researchers describe as the "perverse effects" of spurring on some people to consume more than they normally would (Downs et al., 2009). How could that be?

The city burghers had made a simple, but incorrect, assumption: that informing someone that the double cheeseburger and large fries they had planned on eating contained 930 calories would make them think, "Wow! That's almost half my recommended daily calorie intake. I think I'll have a single burger instead." The fact is that most people are unaware that the average person should consume about 2,000 calories a day in a healthy diet (unless he or she happens to be a lumberjack, in which case it is more like 6,000; at last count, there are not a lot of lumberjacks in Manhattan). So our young man in the burger restaurant, ignorant, as most people are, of the metrics of daily nutrition, might well have thought, seeing that his chosen meal contained 930 calories: "Wow! That sounds impressive. I think I'll have two!"

The calorie information that the restaurants posted had been entirely accurate. But lacking the context within which to interpret it—information about recommended daily intake—it made no sense to most of the people who read it. And, as we saw, the initiative actually backfired. Duke University psychology professor John Payne has coined a term to describe information that does not make sense to the intended target: he says such information lacks "affective ease." If the young man had been told, "The double cheeseburger and large fries will give you 930 calories, which is almost half your recommended intake of calories," he would have been able immediately to understand the situation. The statement has affective ease. However, the information architects in New York City's Department of Health had done a poor job of communication—the information they provided had been correct, but it lacked affective ease. It didn't communicate useful information to its target audience. As a result, the restaurant patrons didn't change their behavior in the way they had been expected to.

Plan sponsors, therefore, have to be good information architects as well as good choice architects. I'll make the point here with one example. It is a universally acknowledged fact that people find it very difficult, even impossible, to emotionally identify with their future selves, especially when that self might be projected thirty-five years into the future, gray-haired, not exactly physically spry, and heading into retirement. This psychological disconnection between present and future selves contributes to the reluctance many young people feel about sacrificing enjoyable spending today and instead putting money into a retirement account for tomorrow. Prudent though such saving is, to the young mind it can feel like giving money to a stranger in the future. And you will read in Chapter 3 that brain-imaging studies show graphically that this is precisely how certain centers in our brains process information about our future selves: as little more than strangers. Who would want to make sacrifices for that old geezer?

How can information architecture help in this case? While he was at Stanford, Hal Hershfield initiated a project designed to help people close the disconnect between their present and future selves; specifically, to help people *emotionally engage* with their future selves. Hershfield subsequently moved to New York University, and the project has attracted extensive collaboration from half a dozen prominent psychologists and behavioral finance experts. And little wonder, for the endeavor looks like something out of *Star Trek* or some such sci-fi enterprise. The idea is simple enough: enable people to see what they will physically look like when they reach retirement, and enable them to observe how their future selves respond emotionally to their present-day decisions about retirement saving behavior. The goal is to close the psychological gap between present and future selves, thus diminishing a serious psychological challenge in the present to saving for retirement.

You can find details about how this magical time travel is achieved (it involves immersive virtual-reality environments, digital age-progression software, and what we call the Face Tool) in Chapter 3. Suffice it to say here that when people make the acquaintance of their aged "selves," they become significantly more willing to begin saving for retirement, and to save more, than individuals who haven't had the experience. The nature of the information we are dealing with in this context is less tangible than, say, calorie counts, but it is obviously highly salient and emotionally engaging. That's what information architects are aiming for. You will see other examples of information architecture in action in Chapter 6 (bringing the reality of retirement life vividly to mind) and Chapter 9 (helping people focus on the future results of their present-day saving, rather than obsessing on short-term distractions). Collectively, Chapters 3, 6, and 9 describe what we call Behavioral Time Machines.

This vivid example demonstrates that the behavioral approach to solving the behavioral challenges of the ailing 401(k) system really does work. It offers a clear vision of the other, similarly based behavioral interventions to come in the following chapters. This new approach became necessary because the traditional attempts to solve these problems—financial education and incentives (primarily, employer matching funds)—have largely failed. One of the reasons for their failure is how they were applied. They were not designed to engage employees so that doing the right thing was easy for them. When we place financial information and incentives in the framework of behavioral architecture, they can indeed be effective, as we will demonstrate in the chapters that follow.

The goal of *Save More Tomorrow*, then, is to enable employers to be wise behavioral architects, not only for their employees but also for themselves. By judiciously applying the behavioral tools presented in the body of the book, employers and their financial advisers can help their workers successfully navigate the behavioral challenges of the retirement plan journey. And by offering an attractive plan, employers can attract the talent they need.

Ours is an ambitious goal, but it is achievable.

COUNTERARGUMENTS

Ambitious goals often provoke resistance because, by their nature, they go beyond familiar territory. We therefore expect that not everyone will agree with everything we present. Each chapter will end with legitimate counterarguments that might be raised, and our responses to them. Here we will address what is perhaps an overarching counterargument to the behavioral approach, namely, that it is excessively paternalistic.

Our response to that charge is simple, yet, we believe, profound. When people are faced with a choice, the environment around that choice will inevitably influence their behavior. In other words, *there is no neutral design* (Thaler and Sunstein, 2009; Benartzi et al., forthcoming). Recall how much influence the way food is displayed in the school cafeteria has on children's lunch choices: if salad is displayed prominently, children will eat more salad, because the children will put on their tray what is easiest and most convenient. If, however, hamburgers are up front, they will eat more hamburgers. The cafeteria manager is a choice architect who simply cannot avoid influencing what children eat for lunch. Period.

Plan sponsors and their advisers are like that cafeteria manager: how they display plan options will strongly influence employees' choices for their retirement future, and they will usually opt for what is easiest and most convenient. In the case of 401(k) plans, the default option is the easiest decision path for the employee, because the employee doesn't have to actively *do* anything. When the plan sponsor sets the default to opt-in, many people will not enroll in the plan because making that decision is hard. When the plan sponsor sets the default to opt-out, everyone will initially be plan participants, and those who don't wish to be in the plan can opt out. I will repeat that short, but profound, five-word phrase: there is no neutral design. How the plan sponsor selects the default option will inevitably influence the retirement futures of all the employees.

When we accept that there is no neutral design, our next task is to ask: What is the most sensible way to set the default? We decided to consult the experts, financial advisers whose professional focus is finding the best strategies for achieving financial security in retirement. We asked them to tell us what percentage of workers they thought should enroll in a retirement savings plan. The answer was, almost everyone—90 percent. The most effective way to achieve that goal is to set the default option as opt-out. Everyone is automatically a saver, and those people who would rather be spenders have the freedom to opt out at any time.

So, to the suggestion that the path we are proposing is paternalistic, our response is: guilty as charged. But we would rather be paternalistic in helping people achieve their desired retirement goals (opt-out), than in making it hard for people to reach those goals (opt-in). Cultivating good eating habits in children is laudable, of course. And cultivating good saving habits in employees, so that they will have a financially secure retirement, is equally laudable.

There is a counterarguments section at the end of all but the final chapter. Our hope is to address objections or difficulties that plan sponsors and their advisers might encounter around the behavioral solutions presented in each chapter. One common counterargument is, "My plan provider is unable to implement the recommended behavioral solution." We recognize that all of us involved in the goal to improve the 401(k) world—we, the behavioralists, you, the plan sponsors and advisers—are at the cutting edge of applying the new science of behavioral finance to practical problems. Inevitably, some in the 401(k) world have yet to catch up to the future, so to speak, and as yet are what we might call Behavioral-Finance challenged, or BeFi-challenged. Our advice to plan sponsors who find their plan providers BeFi-challenged is simple: it is in your interests and the interests of your employees to find a plan provider who is BeFi-capable.

THE 90—10—90 PLANSUCCESS GOALS

The bulk of *Save More Tomorrow*—Chapters 1 through 9—describes behavioral solutions to behavioral problems around joining, saving, and investing in 401(k) plans, and the practical implementation of those solutions. The final chapter, Chapter 10, shows how we put this behavioral finance toolbox to work, using what we call the PlanSuccess Behavioral Audit. The Plan-Success System is the process by which we implement and monitor the ongoing success of the behavioral finance intervention, with the goal of creating behaviorally healthy retirement plans.

By our definition, behaviorally healthy plans have high participation, adequate savings levels, and a wise investment strategy. In order to obtain appropriate numbers for these elements of retirement planning, we conducted two surveys of 401(k) experts, using the same set of questions in each case. The first group was the nineteen attendees of the Allianz Global Investors Retirement Summit, held in Dallas in May 2011. The second group was 115 attendees at the Center for Due Diligence Advisor Conference in Chicago, October 2011. We asked them about optimal plan participation, savings level, and investment options. (See Appendix 1 for the list of questions.) Based on these combined responses, and supplemented by academic literature on a savings rate necessary to provide 80 percent income replacement (Ibbotson et al., 2007), we are recommending the following target goals for plan sponsors:

- A plan participation rate of 90 percent.
- An individual savings rate of at least 10 percent. (This assumes a generous employer match. In the absence of such a match, the individual savings rate should be higher.)
- Ninety percent of participants have their assets invested in a target-date fund, or other one-stop, professionally managed portfolio solutions.

We recognize that while many—perhaps most—companies have the potential to reach the "90—10—90" goals, some will not, not because they are not doing the right thing, but because of employee demographics. For instance, some low-income employees may be struggling financially and are simply unable to save, even if they want to. Companies with a high proportion of such employees are unlikely to achieve 90 percent plan participation, even if behaviorally they are doing the right thing, such as having automatic enrollment. At the other end of the employee demographic, companies with a high proportion of financially literate employees will probably not reach 90 percent of plan participants opting for a one-stop portfolio solution. Such employees are likely to prefer to construct their own portfolios.

A word here about industry benchmarking with respect to these numbers. Plan sponsors often have the very understandable tendency to compare the performance of their own retirement plans to the industry average. It is very tempting to be pleased, and even satisfied, if one's own participation rate is a little above industry average, say, 72 percent as compared to 70 percent. But being slightly above a figure that is widely considered by behavioralists as being woefully inadequate is nothing to be proud of. We are saying that by becoming wise behavioral architects, plan sponsors will find it surprisingly easy to do a lot better than the industry average in all measures of plan behavioral health. We are urging them to be more ambitious, and to do the right things for themselves and their employees.

STRUCTURE OF THE BOOK

Four sections follow the introduction.

The first three address the three key actions employees must take on their retirement plan journeys:

- Section 1: Deciding to enroll in a 401(k) plan. (Save)
- Section 2: Selecting an adequate savings rate. (Save More)
- Section 3: Making wise investment decisions. (Save Smarter)

Each section will contain three chapters dealing with the key behavioral challenges—inertia, loss aversion, and myopia—and the appropriate behavioral solutions. Each chapter begins with a preview, which is effectively an executive summary. These nine chapters are shown in the 3 x 3 challenge/solution matrix on the next page. While the matrix is a logical organization for the book, it does not imply that each cell within it, each chapter, is isolated. Inevitably, there are interactions among them. For instance, many solutions we propose for increasing participation might also increase savings. Equally, many solutions we propose for increasing savings might also increase participation.

The single major chapter in the fourth section describes the concept and implementation of the PlanSuccess Behavioral Audit we have developed to determine the behavioral health of plans, and how the behavioral solutions may be applied to improve the situation, moving toward the 90—10—90 goals. It presents the experience of one company, Orbitz Worldwide, Inc., as a case study. Concluding remarks follow.

— Chapter Matrix of Decision Challenges and Behavioral Solutions —

	Design Easy Choices to Address Inertia	Manage Losses to Address Loss Aversion	Provide Behavioral Time Machines to Address Myopia
Save	**Chapter 1. Auto-Takeoff:** Change default to automatic enrollment to address inertia and increase participation.	**Chapter 2. Match Optimizer:** Re-optimize employer match to encourage more participation without costing the employer a lot more. Employees will be saving more.	**Chapter 3. The Face Tool:** Help people see their future selves, through digital age-morphing, so they will be willing to begin saving for their retirement years.
Save More	**Chapter 4. Save More Tomorrow 1.0:** Invite employees to pre-commit to automatic saving increases, thus avoiding the problem of inertia and procrastination.	**Chapter 5. Save More Tomorrow 2.0:** Arrange savings rate increases to coincide with salary increases, thus avoiding loss aversion.	**Chapter 6. Imagine Exercise:** Help people bring to mind their specific wishes for a comfortable retirement, so they will be willing to save more for their retirement years.
Save Smarter	**Chapter 7. Investment Solutions Pyramid:** Offer different investment options, based on participants' preferences. The expectation is that 90 percent of participants will invest in a professionally managed portfolio, such as target date funds.	**Chapter 8. Lifetime Statement:** Change the "quarterly statement" to "Lifetime Statement," and put long-term performance on page one in place of short-term performance. Participants become longer-term investors.	**Chapter 9. Tangible Account Statement:** Change account statements to reflect projected monthly income at retirement. Participants will then find it easy to know if they are on track with saving and investing.

Figure i–1.

A Note about Fees

The practical thrust of *Save More Tomorrow*, then, is the pressing need for plan sponsors and advisers to conduct a behavioral audit of their plans. It goes without saying that they should also conduct a fiduciary audit to ensure that participants are not paying excessive fees, for instance, because fees can be a significant drain on ultimate accumulation. Even a small difference in investment fees can have a dramatic impact on outcomes, as illustrated by a recent report by the Government Accounting Office (GAO). A one-half of a percentage point in additional plan expenses over a thirty-year period reduces ultimate accumulation by 13 percent (GAO, 2006). These small annual numbers have a big impact in the long term.

Transparency around fees is a perennial concern, with disclosures often being so arcane or convoluted that deciphering them is a challenge. It is therefore not surprising that most plan participants apparently have only a rudimentary understanding of fees. For instance, a recent survey asked plan participants if they paid fees for their 401(k) plans. Almost two-thirds replied that they did not and only 17 percent said they do (AARP, 2007).

Clearly, plan sponsors and their advisers need to be vigilant about fees. However, there are many tools available to plan sponsors and advisers to help them cope with this important issue. Fees are therefore not within the scope of this book.

BEGINNING THE JOURNEY: RETIREMENT PLANES

We can think of people's passage through their working lives, ending with an adequately funded retirement, as akin to a journey with a desired destination:

- The employee will enroll in his company's retirement savings plans early on.
- The employee will gradually increase savings to reach an adequate level.
- The employee will invest wisely, enjoying her lifetime savings during retirement years and avoiding outliving her savings.

We offer the analogy of a plane trip for this journey toward retirement:

▶ The act of enrolling in a retirement plan is the **takeoff** for the journey. The alternative—not joining a plan—would leave our (misguided) employee **grounded**, stranded at the terminal, going nowhere.

The employee can then ask, Would I prefer to be offered a retirement plan in which enrollment is automatic (which we call **Auto-Takeoff**), or is it better to have to take steps to be enrolled, with the very strong likelihood that I would end up not participating (or **Auto-Grounded**)?

▶ The gradual increase in annual savings rate is the plane's **climb** toward cruising altitude. The (misguided) employees who elect not to increase their savings rate would be like a plane caught in a **holding** pattern, unable to achieve cruising altitude.

The employee can now ask, Would I appreciate a plan in which savings increases are automatic (**Auto-Climb**), or should that responsibility be left to the individual, with the very strong likelihood that adequate savings rate will not be reached (or **Auto-Holding**)?

▶ The responsibility for managing the growing portfolio throughout an employee's working life is, of course, crucial to achieving the desired target accumulation. The employee can elect to have a professional assume that responsibility, in which case the portfolio will be managed by experts, and enjoy a **smooth** ride. The (misguided) employees who elect to manage their account assets themselves, and in all likelihood not do a very good job, will suffer a **turbulent** ride.

Finally, the employee asks, Would I prefer to have the fund's growing assets be professionally managed (**Auto-Smooth**), or would I want to take on that responsibility myself, with the very strong likelihood that investment returns would be more erratic than they should be (or **Auto-Turbulent**)?

▶ Like takeoff, landing a plane is among the most dangerous of all the maneuvers on the journey. The same is true for the prudent handling of a retirement fund: no matter how good the accumulation phase has been, a misguided decumulation procedure could be disastrous. So employees have the choice to select a **safe landing** or a very distressing **crash landing**.*

The Retirement Plane Journey

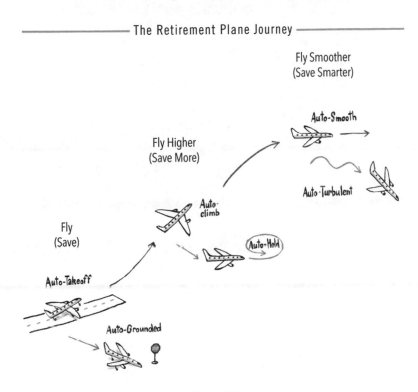

Figure i–2.

These are the key issues that occupy us in the three main sections of the book: joining a plan, choosing an appropriate rate of saving, and wise portfolio selection. Each involves behavioral

---

* Management of the decumulation phase of the retirement program will be covered in a future book.

challenges, as we saw earlier. And each has behavioral solutions, as you will see in detail as you go through the book. These behavioral solutions are designed to make the processes as easy as possible for employers and employees and to be in the best interests of all involved.

Bon Voyage!

REFERENCES

AARP. 2007. "401(k) Participants' Awareness and Understanding of Fees."

Benartzi, Shlomo. 2011. *Behavioral Finance in Action*. Allianz Global Investors, Center for Behavioral Finance.

Benartzi, Shlomo, and Richard H. Thaler. 1999. "Risk Aversion or Myopia? Choices in Repeated Gambles and Retirement Investments." *Management Science* 45, no. 3: 364–81.

———. 2001. "Naïve Diversification Strategies in Defined Contribution Saving Plans." *American Economic Review* 91, no. 1: 79–98.

———. 2007. "Heuristics and Biases in Retirement Savings Behavior." *Journal of Economic Perspectives* 21, no. 3: 81–104.

Benartzi, Shlomo, Ehud Peleg, and Richard H. Thaler. Forthcoming. "Choice Architecture and Retirement Saving Plans," in *The Behavioral Foundations of Policy*, edited by Eldar Shafir. New Jersey: Princeton University Press.

Choi, James J., David Laibson, Brigitte C. Madrian, and Andrew Metrick. 2006. "Defined Contribution Pensions: Plan Rules, Participant Decisions, and the Path of Least Resistance." In *Tax Policy and the Economy*, vol. 16, edited by James Poterba. Cambridge: MIT Press.

Downs, Julie S., George Loewenstein, and Jessica Wisdom. 2009. "Strategies for Promoting Healthier Food Choices." *American Economic Review* 99, no. 2: 1–10.

Employee Benefits Research Institute. 2007. "Retirement Trends in the United States over the Past Quarter Century," *Facts from EBRI*.

Financial Engines. 2011. *401(k) Plan Survey*.

GAO. 2006. *Changes Needed to Provide 401(k) Plan Participants and the Department of Labor Better Information*.

Hancock Financial Services. 2002. *Insight into Participant Investment Knowledge and Behavior*.

Ibbotson, Roger, James Xiong, Robert Kreitler, Charles Kreitlet, and Peng Chen. 2007. "National Savings Rate Guidelines for Individuals." *Journal of Financial Planning* (April): 50–61.

Kahneman, Daniel. 2003. "Maps of Bounded Rationality: Psychology for Behavioral Economics." *The American Economic Review* 93, no. 5: 1449–75.

———. 2011. *Thinking, Fast and Slow*. Farrar, Straus and Giroux.

Poterba, James, et al. 2007. "New Estimates of the Future Path of 401(k) Assets." National Bureau of Economic Research, Working Paper No. 13083.

PSCA. 2011. "54th Annual Survey."

Thaler, Richard H., and Shlomo Benartzi. 2004. "Save More Tomorrow: Using Behavioral Economics to Increase Employee Savings." *Journal of Political Economy* 112, no. 1, part 2: S164–87.

Thaler, Richard H., and Cass R. Sunstein. 2009. *Nudge: Improving Decisions About Health, Wealth, and Happiness.* New York: Penguin.

TIAA-CREF company history. http://www.tiaa-cref.org/public/about/press/about_us/company-history/index.html.

Zweig, Jason. 1998. "How the Big Brains Invest at TIAA-CREF." *Money* (January): 118.

SAVE

90—10—90 GOALS

Under traditional Auto-Grounded 401(k) plans, new hires are very slow to join, and even after three years of tenure almost one-third have still failed to join. For most people, participating in a retirement savings plan is a wise decision, because, apart from Social Security, they will have few financial resources with which to secure a comfortable retirement. The three chapters in this section describe behavioral interventions designed to overcome the behavioral challenges of inertia, loss aversion, and myopia that together are largely responsible for low participation rates. The question we pose here is: what target level of participation may be described as behaviorally healthy?

We approached this question in two ways. First, we sought the opinion of 401(k) plan specialists. We asked the 134 401(k) experts in the two surveys mentioned in the introductory chapter, What percentage of employees with access to a 401(k) plan should enroll? We combined their answers, which were uniformly high: the average was 97.25, with a median of 100.

Second, we looked at studies of participation levels in 401(k) plans that include the Auto-Takeoff feature, with the freedom to opt out at any time. We reasoned that this would indicate at least what is attainable in the real world. Given that participants are able to opt out at any time, one can also tentatively assume that the proportion of participants who remain in the plan after, say, three years represents the collective wish to save. It could be argued, of course, that the default opt-out feature "tricks" employees into being plan participants when they would rather not be, but remain so because of inertia. We demonstrate in the first chapter of the section that this is not the case.

When we looked at studies of 401(k) plans with Auto-Takeoff we found pretty high participation rates, indeed, almost as high as those recommended by our 401(k) specialists. For instance, one study of four plans with Auto-Takeoff reported a range of participation of 86 to 96 percent at six months, with only a slight rise in subsequent years (Choi et al., 2004). A Vanguard study of forty-eight plans with Auto-Takeoff found a somewhat lower figure, showing an average participation of 86 percent (Vanguard, 2007). These two averages, of 91 and 86 percent, tell us that high participation is achievable in the real world, and (we believe) that almost all employees want to save for retirement.

Given these two sets of data, we are electing to recommend a participation rate of 90 percent. We could have recommended a lower number, say the 70 percent average participation rate that is typical in 401(k) plans, but why recommend such a low number when many more employees seem to want to save? Similarly, why recommend just 70 percent when a much higher participation rate is attainable using behavioral finance lessons, as we will illustrate in the next chapters.

We also could have pushed the 90 percent higher to, say, the 97.25 average participation rates recommended by the 401(k) specialists we surveyed. However, we realize that some employers will not be able to reach such a high participation rate with their specific employee demographics, and we felt setting an unattainable goal could end up demotivating employers trying to set up a healthy 401(k) plan.

As behavioralists, we admit that we were also seeking a simple, powerful heuristic, or rule of thumb, for our PlanSuccess goals, because we know that people respond positively to such devices. At least one consumer behavior expert tells us that 90—10—90 has the *feel* of such a rule of thumb (Payne, 2011).

In the following three chapters you will learn about the behavioral interventions that will enable employers and employees to attain the first of the three (90—10—90) PlanSuccess goals.

REFERENCES

Choi, James J., David Laibson and Brigitte C. Madrian. 2004. "Plan Design and 401(k) Savings Outcomes." *National Tax Journal* 57, pp 275–98.

Payne, John, personal communication, 2011.

Vanguard, 2007. "Measuring the Effectiveness of Automatic Enrollment," December.

CHAPTER 1

AUTO-TAKEOFF

PREVIEW

Despite the widespread recognition among workers of the wisdom of saving for retirement, almost one-third of those who are eligible to participate in employer-sponsored 401(k) plans fail to do so. In a majority of such plans, employees must take active steps to opt in in order to enroll (following our Retirement Plane journey analogy, we describe those who fail to join as being Auto-Grounded).

Electing whether or not to join a retirement plan should be a no-brainer, given that most people say they don't want to live in poverty when they are older. In addition, joining a plan has significant tax advantages and, in most cases, the benefit of employer matching funds. But looming large over this apparently simple yes/no decision are complexities and uncertainties surrounding saving and investment decisions, and these have a major impact on employees' behavior around what should be the simple act of enrolling in a plan.

Deciding how much to save initially, with an eye to increasing the rate as time passes, and selecting a wise investment portfolio are extremely challenging tasks. Most people are simply not equipped to calculate how much they need to save each year in order to have adequate funds to secure a comfortable retirement. And, as we saw in the Introduction, people easily become confused when faced with a large number of investment options succumb to choice overload, and often end up making no selection at all.

Faced with the multiple complexities surrounding saving and investment, many people feel overwhelmed and become unable to make what should be the simple yes/no decision about enrolling. Instead they turn to "coping strategies." These include going with the default option of doing nothing and deciding to put off the decision until later. Procrastination often ultimately leads to the default option. As a result, far too many people find themselves not saving for their retirement, in other words being Auto-Grounded.

A simple but powerful behavioral solution to this challenge is to change the choice architecture around enrollment: specifically, change the default option to opt-out (we call this Auto-Takeoff). Under this system, new (and existing) employees are automatically enrolled in the company's retirement plan, with a carefully designed default savings rate and asset allocation. Plan participants may opt out at any time they wish. However, plan sponsors must repeatedly ask those employees who opt out when they would like to enroll in the future, a mechanism called "Future Enrollment." This new choice architecture makes enrollment easy for employees, and plan participation dramatically increases.

THE POWER OF THE DEFAULT OPTION

Employers are not required by law to offer retirement plans to their employees, yet many do, often motivated by the wish to "do the right thing" for them. (A generous retirement plan might also be an effective tool for attracting talent in a competitive labor market.) Employers therefore have an interest in finding ways to encourage their people to participate in a retirement plan. What can employers do? Three broad classes of intervention are open to them: providing financial information, providing incentives (employer matching funds), and plan design.

We saw in the introductory chapter that incentives and efforts at education are not as effective as was expected. Here we offer an alternate, behavioral solution: change the choice architecture so that employees are automatically enrolled in the plan, with a default savings rate and asset allocation, but are free to opt out at any time. (However, as we will see shortly, employers should take steps to encourage those who opt out to enroll in the future.)

By way of illustrating the power of the default option, I will describe its impact in an entirely different context, that of registering for organ donation.

According to standard economic theory, defaults should have only a limited effect on people's decisions: theory says that if a default is not aligned with people's preferences, they will choose otherwise. That is obviously not the case, as the organ donation registration story reveals dramatically (Johnson and Goldstein, 2003). A 1993 Gallup Poll reported that 85 percent of Americans approve of organ donation, and yet only 28 percent actively take the steps to register as a donor. As a result, in the United States almost 6,000 people die every year waiting for a suitable donor organ. A similar disparity between expressed preference and subsequent action exists in several European countries.

An even more significant disparity, however, is seen in the effective consent rates in various countries within Europe, countries that often are neighbors and share similar cultural backgrounds. For instance, the consent rate in Germany is 12 percent, whereas in neighboring Austria it is a staggering 99.98 percent. The difference between these two countries is the choice architecture surrounding consent: Germans have to opt in to the system to become potential donors (most don't); Austrians, by contrast, are assumed to be willing donors, unless they actively opt out (most don't). (See Figure 1-1.)

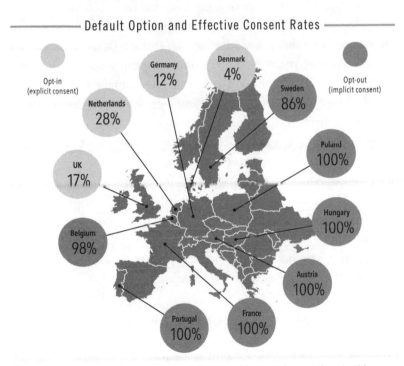

—————— Default Option and Effective Consent Rates ——————

Opt-in
(explicit consent)

Opt-out
(implicit consent)

Germany
12%

Denmark
4%

Sweden
86%

Netherlands
28%

Poland
100%

UK
17%

Hungary
100%

Belgium
98%

Austria
100%

Portugal
100%

France
100%

Figure 1-1. Because of inertia, most people stay with the default option. In this case, those countries with opt-in consent for organ donation have a low effective consent rate. Equally, those countries with an opt-out default see very high effective consent rates. (Adapted from: *Do Defaults Save Lives?* by Eric J. Johnson and Daniel Goldstein, 2003. Reprinted with permission from AAAS.)

In both countries, the default option is what most people are doing, but in one the choice architecture automatically decreases the number of potential donors, whereas in the other the number of potential donors dramatically increases. You can see from the numbers in the figure that the default (opt-out) option in this case is not only effective at boosting donor pool membership, it is *extremely* powerful.

One interesting parallel between the organ donor registration experience in Europe and participation in 401(k) plans in the United States (and elsewhere, for that matter) comes from the Netherlands, in the realm of the efficacy of education. In 1998 the Dutch government established a national donor registry. It launched an extensive education program, which included sending out 12 million letters (in a country with a population of 15.8 million) urging people to register. As with many financial education programs in the retirement plan context, much to the Dutch government's surprise and disappointment, their education campaign for organ donor registration did little to influence people's *actions*. Offering the right default option is obviously more efficacious than supplying educational information, no matter how pertinent it may be.

Given these stark realities about the impact of choice architecture on organ donor registration in various European countries, there is no prize for guessing which default option operates in the United States. As Johnson and Goldstein say in the conclusion to their now classic paper, "Policy makers . . . should consider that defaults make a difference."

THE IMPACT OF AUTO-TAKEOFF ON PLAN PARTICIPATION

Given what you have seen with the choice architecture around registering for organ donation, I am sure you would predict that shifting from standard, Auto-Grounded enrollment for 401(k) plans to Auto-Takeoff would dramatically increase employee participation. You would be correct.

During the past decade, more than a dozen studies have been carried out on the impact of Auto-Takeoff on employee participation in employer-sponsored retirement plans. The first was by Brigitte Madrian and Dennis Shea, published in 2001, and it caught people's attention with its cogent results that showed sharply increased participation (Madrian and Shea, 2001). Reaction to this first test of changing the default in the real world of 401(k) plans was mixed. There were many skeptical voices that said, essentially, "If people aren't signing up for retirement plans, there must be a good reason" (Madrian, 2011). However, every subsequent study delivered the same message: as with organ donor registration, the Auto-Takeoff default option is not only effective, it is extremely powerful. There was a good reason why people weren't signing up in the traditional opt-in plans. But it wasn't the reason the skeptics had in mind.

I will describe just one of the studies, which focused on a medium-sized U.S. chemicals company that first adopted Auto-Takeoff in December of 2000 (Beshears et al., 2009). Prior to that date the company had a standard, and relatively generous, defined-contribution savings plan: employees could defer up to 15 percent of pay into the plan; the employer matched the employees' contributions dollar-for-dollar up to 6 percent of pay; and employees had seven investment options from which to choose. This company's case is especially interesting, because it implemented Auto-Takeoff in two different ways, which yielded important extra insight into the dynamics of Auto-Takeoff.

When the company adopted Auto-Takeoff in 2000, it set a default contribution rate at 3 percent of pay, which applied not only to new hires but also to existing, non-participating employees. Almost a year later, the default rate was increased to 6 percent, applicable only to new employees. The outcomes were quite clear-cut. Participation for employees hired before Auto-Takeoff was adopted was low initially, and increased slowly as tenure increased. By contrast, under Auto-Takeoff participation

——————————— Automatic Enrollment and Plan Participation ———————————

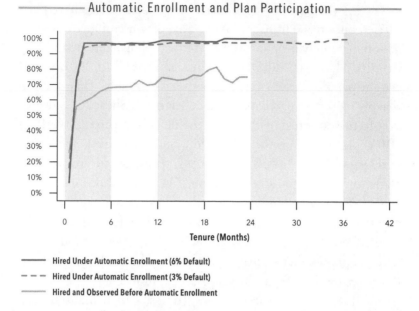

——— Hired Under Automatic Enrollment (6% Default)
– – – Hired Under Automatic Enrollment (3% Default)
——— Hired and Observed Before Automatic Enrollment

Figure 1-2. Automatic enrollment in a 401(k) plan (auto-takeoff) gives an immediate and substantial boost to participation, and employees who are required to opt in (auto-grounded) never attain the same level of participation. Here we see virtually identical participation rates with 3 and 6 percent default saving rates. (Source: "The Importance of Default Options for Retirement Savings Outcomes" by John Beshears, James J. Choi, David Laibson, and Brigitte C. Madian, in Jeffrey R. Brown, Jeffery B. Liebman, and David A. Wise, eds., *Social Security Policy in a Changing Environment.* University of Chicago Press, 2009.)

jumped to close to 95 percent as soon as it took effect (between one and two months, in this case), and subsequently increased only slightly. The difference in participation between Auto-Grounded and Auto-Takeoff employees at three months was some 35 percentage points—60 compared with 95 percent. After two years, that gap had narrowed somewhat, to 70 compared with 95 percent. Participation under the traditional Auto-Grounded system never reached what is typically immediately achieved under Auto-Takeoff. This is a spectacular result by any measure, just as we see with every instance of adoption of Auto-Takeoff: employees join sooner, and more of them join eventually.

This company's case is especially interesting because it provides a natural experiment on the impact of the default savings rate on participation. Some observers had assumed that a relatively high initial savings rate (6 percent in this case) might cause more employees to opt out than with a lower rate (3 percent). In fact, the opt-out rates were virtually identical in both cohorts. The higher default savings rate (at least, in this range) did not prompt a greater number of people to opt out, so the participation rate was the same in both cases. (See Figure 1-2.)

Why does the Auto-Takeoff default option work so well? First, because people say they want to save (Choi et al., 2006). Second, Auto-Takeoff *makes it easy* for them to participate.

THE IMPORTANCE OF EARLY ENROLLMENT

The ultimate rate of participation is of prime importance, obviously. But the fact that participation occurs almost immediately after a new employee joins the company under Auto-Takeoff, rather than after a lag of three to five years, as often happens under the Auto-Grounded system, is important, too. Those "lost" few years at the beginning of a thirty-five-year investment program have a significant financial impact down the line, because of the power of compound growth. By way of illustration, here is the story of two hypothetical employees, "Brian" and "Randy," chums from high school who both joined "Tekk-Corp Inc." on January 1, 2010, both thirty years old at the time.

Brian and Randy were technically sophisticated and each earned $60,000 when they joined the company. They both intended to retire when they reached sixty-five. Brian, who was married and had two small children, was the more serious of the two. He immediately signed up for TekkCorp's 401(k) plan, saving 6 percent of his pay, which was matched by the company, fifty cents on the dollar, up to 6 percent. Party-boy Randy would have none of his friend's "sensible" savings strategy, and preferred to buy his dream car and have a good time. Five years later, with marriage and children in view, Randy decided that being "sensible" was not so stupid after all, and opted into Tekk-Corp's 401(k) plan on the same terms as his pal. Here is what Brian and Randy would have accumulated when they reached sixty-five, assuming a 7 percent annual return on their investments (and, for simplicity of calculation, no change in salary):

- Brian: $773,000
- Randy: $528,000

Randy realized, too late, that his penchant for partying for just a few years in his youth now meant that he would have to live on a retirement income that was just two-thirds the size of his pal's. Or, if he wanted to be as comfortable as Brian, face the necessity of working five years longer than he had planned, which would mean retirement at seventy years of age. Not a happy prospect. Signing up promptly is *very* important.

THE IMPLEMENTATION OF AUTO-TAKEOFF

When the company that Madrian and Shea studied back in the late 1990s introduced Auto-Takeoff, it wasn't the first in the United States to do so, but the practice was relatively uncommon at the time. Sources vary on the percentage of companies that offer Auto-Takeoff, but an average of three major sources for 2009 gives 40 percent of new hires in large plans, 30 percent in mid-size plans, and 11 percent for small plans (GAO, 2009). Increases in the adoption rate have been quite rapid in recent years, but that rate has slowed significantly of late (GAO, 2009; PSCA, 2010; Vanguard, 2010). Part of the reason for its increased prevalence in the United States is a provision in the 2006 Pension Protection Act, which offers legal protections and business incentives to companies that switch to Auto-Takeoff. Similar provisions have been enacted in New Zealand with the KiwiSaver Act of 2006 and in the United Kingdom with the Pensions Act of 2007.

Evidently, Auto-Takeoff has been catching on, although it still has a long way to go, especially with the recent slowing in new adoptions. It has a long way to go, not just in the implementation of this plan feature, but also in the savings rate and investment strategies that are applied. For instance, most companies that have adopted Auto-Takeoff have opted for a rather low initial default savings rate, typically around 3 percent. Many such plan sponsors say they fear that higher defaults will cause automatically enrolled participants to opt out, thus undermining the whole point of the system. There are, however, two behavioral challenges at play here: one for the employee, the other for the employer.

When employees are automatically enrolled in a plan with a 3 percent savings rate, most are very slow to increase it, for two reasons. First, the employee might take the default rate as tacit advice, and simply stay with it. Second, and more important, just as inertia powerfully guides employees to be in an Auto-Takeoff retirement plan by default, so, too, does it lead them to be passive savers. Status quo wins the day, and people don't increase their level of saving unless prompted to do so. (You will read about one powerful program to achieve that goal in Chapters 4 and 5). Inertia also traps most employees in their initial asset allocation, and even university professors who should know better often do not rebalance their portfolios for years or even decades (Madrian and Shea, 2001; Beshears et al., 2009; Samuelson and Zeckhauser, 1988). We offer behavioral solutions to these investment challenges in Chapter 7.

Employers also face a behavioral challenge over the initial default savings rate. Although, as we saw earlier, many voice their concern that too high a rate might cause their employees to opt out of the plan, inertia and the related status quo bias are also in play for the employer. Given a retirement savings landscape in which the initial default rate is typically 3 percent, most employers see no compelling reason to choose a higher figure and stand out on the retirement plan landscape as something of an oddity. This status quo bias acts powerfully, despite the fact that the ultimate savings rate goal that is most commonly recommended by financial advisers is at least three times that figure. Inertia keeps the 3 percent figure in plain sight on the landscape. Employers go with it, and their employees stick with it, to their detriment.

We, however, are going to be more ambitious, and propose a 6 percent initial default savings rate, for two reasons. First, because, as we saw with the case of the chemicals company earlier, there are essentially identical participation rates among new hires when the default is 3 percent or 6 percent, with identical employer match rates. Second, and most important, because going with the higher initial default rate helps employees get to the ultimate goal of 10 percent much faster.

This, then, is the implementation of Auto-Takeoff. Employers automatically enroll new and existing employees in their 401(k) plans, with the prescribed default savings rate of 6 percent of pay, and a well-diversified portfolio. Employees do not have to face the complexity of decisions about savings and investment, because these decisions are set for them, so they can feel comfortable with the default enrollment option. In this case, inertia works in the employees' best interests, because the default option means they will be saving for their retirement, which is what most people say they want. Auto-Takeoff makes participating in a retirement plan as easy as it can possibly be, from the employee's point of view.

There will be a small proportion of employees who will opt

out, of course, for any one of a variety of reasons. They might feel they have no reason to save, for instance, or they don't want to start saving right now, or, more likely, they are simply procrastinating. Put bluntly, they lack sufficient self-control to do the right thing now, and they are not alone.

Few of us have the self-control of a nun, though perhaps we would wish to. We can think of self-control as being akin to a healthy bank account that always remains just out of reach. There is a little self-control in the account today, we reluctantly recognize that, but we are confident that it will be flush in the near future. We can think of a big dose of self-control being deposited in the account each month, akin to a paycheck periodically swelling our account. But, as with the paycheck, self-control depletes at an alarming rate, and we are once again in possession of way too little self-control to be good for us. Too often we break that diet, skip a planned visit to the gym, or fail to enroll in a retirement plan, even though we know that doing each one of these things would be in our best interests.

Plan sponsors and financial advisers should therefore not treat the Auto-Takeoff process as a one-time effort to enroll employees. Rather, to maximize participation they should recognize that many employees are struggling with issues of self-control, and need help with that behavioral challenge. They should engage in dialogue with those people who opt out and ask them, "Okay, when would you like to enroll in the plan in the future? Would you like to join next year? Next January?" We call this feature "Future Enrollment," which is the behavioral solution to the challenge of limited self-control. Plan sponsors should put in place a mechanism for annual reminders to the opted-out employees, prompting them to consider enrolling in the plan. Opting out should be viewed as a temporary, short-term contingency on the part of the employee, not as a permanent solution.

COUNTERARGUMENTS

Although adopting Auto-Takeoff appears to be a no-brainer for those who want to see the highest possible employee participation in retirement plans, we anticipate some objections:

Auto-Takeoff is paternalistic.

We explained in the Introduction that when an employer offers options to its employees, an act of paternalism cannot be avoided, if one of the options is a default. The proper approach to this issue, then, is to ask: which is the more appropriate default option in this particular case, Auto-Takeoff or Auto-Grounded?

We gave a moral slant to this question in the Introduction. Here is a quantitative slant: the 2 x 2 "Mistake Matrix," shown on the next page. (See Figure 1-3.) It shows the two default options, Auto-Takeoff and Auto-Grounded. Then we have two kinds of people: those who should be saving (which is 90 percent of workers), because, aside from Social Security, this is likely to be their only source of retirement income, whom we call "Savers"; and those who should not be saving (10 percent of workers), because, for whatever reasons, they cannot, or they have no reason to save, whom we call the "Spenders."

Now we look at the matrix and ask: which default system produces the bigger mistake, Auto-Grounded or Auto-Takeoff? Under the Auto-Grounded system, 20 percent of Savers are making a mistake, because typically only 70 percent actually enroll, whereas 90 percent of them should. Under Auto-Takeoff it is the Spenders who would be making a mistake, if indeed they fail to opt out. However, close to 10 percent of employees who are automatically enrolled typically opt out, which is the figure for employees that our survey shows—again, for whatever reason—will not want to save, and don't. Under Auto-Takeoff, therefore, the great majority of people who don't want to save opt out of the plan, leaving almost no one saving when they would rather be spending.

The answer to the question "Which is the more appropriate default option?" is blindingly clear: it is the Auto-Takeoff option, because this gives by far the fewest employees who find themselves where they don't want to be and close to 0 percent of employees who make the mistake of saving when they would rather be spending. This compares to 20 percent of employees who make the mistake of spending when they would prefer to save, but don't, under the Auto-Grounded plan.

The Mistake Matrix

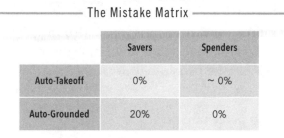

	Savers	Spenders
Auto-Takeoff	0%	~ 0%
Auto-Grounded	20%	0%

Figure 1–3.

The above numbers strongly imply that when people are in an option (in this case, contributing to a 401(k) plan) that they don't like, they correct the situation. They opt out. Another example reinforces this conclusion. In 2006, a British company established a retirement plan with a very aggressive default savings rate of 12 percent, with a one-for-one employer match between 12 and 18 percent of pay. Employees would therefore have to increase their savings substantially above the already high default level to gain any benefit from employer contributions. This is a very unattractive offering, and most people showed their displeasure very quickly. Within twelve months, 75 percent of participants had changed from the default savings rate, mostly to lower figures (Beshears et al., 2010a). People do not passively stay in options they find objectionable. Misguided paternalism therefore cannot force people to go down a path they would rather avoid.

The last point is what employees themselves say about the Auto-Takeoff process. A Harris Interactive poll found that 97 percent of employees who were automatically enrolled in a plan, and who remained in the plan, were satisfied with the process. Equally important: of those who elected to opt out, 90 percent said that they, too, were satisfied. And 95 percent of plan participants agreed that the process had made saving for retirement easy (Harris Interactive Inc., 2007). This is what choice architects like to hear, because their goal is to make it easy for people to do what they say they want to do.

It is still too paternalistic.

If an employer still objects to Auto-Takeoff as too paternalistic despite the above argument, or for any other reason, a low-cost and quite effective alternative is Easy Enroll. This process achieves virtually the same goal as Auto-Takeoff: it makes it easy for employees to achieve what they say they want to achieve, but it does not involve automatic enrollment.

The key to Easy Enroll is, as its name implies, that it must be easy. The enrollment form must be simple, prominently featuring a yes/no decision box. Checking "Yes" would lead to immediate enrollment in a retirement plan with the same parameters as in Auto-Takeoff. The Easy decision could also be made "Active," which adds an extra edge of employee engagement. For instance, during orientation, new hires are required to fill in important forms such as a health insurance option selection form and a direct-deposit form. By physically situating the retirement plan enrollment form between these two other forms, it more effectively demands attention. Employees are invited to fill in the form and hand it in with the other forms when they leave the orientation event.

One study found that this kind of Easy Enroll process resulted in a participation rate of 42 percent after twelve months. This compared with a rate of just 21 percent after twelve months under the standard Auto-Grounded system (Beshears et al., 2010b).

Auto-Takeoff makes no sense in a company with high employee turnover.

This is easily addressed. Offer an Auto-Grounded plan when new employees join, and put in place Auto-Takeoff on people's first anniversary of joining the company. This allows motivated employees to participate immediately upon joining the company, if they so wish. At the same time, it avoids the bureaucratic hassles of dealing with many "orphan" accounts for employees who don't last a full year.

You recommend an initial saving rate of 6 percent, but I find that high, despite your argument that it doesn't lower participation.

If you really can't go with a 6 percent initial saving rate, for whatever reason, consider a slightly lower rate, say 4 or 5 percent.

As an employer, I don't like Auto-Takeoff because it is going to cost me money, through my employer matching contribution.

That is an understandable concern. However, we offer a behaviorally designed employer matching contribution that achieves a higher participation rate but does not cost the employer much more, if anything, in matching funds. We describe this "Match Optimizer" in the following chapter, Chapter 2.

BEHAVIORAL FINANCE ACTIONS

▶**Action 1:** Make participation easy for employees by implementing Auto-Takeoff. Under this plan, every new (and non-participating existing) employee is enrolled in the retirement plan, but is informed that they can opt out at any point, if they wish.

▶**Action 2:** Establish the initial default savings rate at 6 percent. Inform employees that they are free to adjust their savings rate at any time. (See Chapters 4–6 for behavioral finance tools that help employees increase the rate over time.)

▶**Action 3:** Implement Future Enrollment. Engage in dialogue with employees who opt out. Ask them, "When would you like to enroll in the future? Next January? A year from now?" Put a mechanism in place to ask these opted-out employees annually when they would like to enroll in the future.

▶**Action 4:** If for some reason Auto-Takeoff cannot be established, introduce Easy Enroll instead, which has the same default saving and investment options as Auto-Takeoff. Under this feature, during orientation employees are invited to fill out plan enrollment forms with a simple yes/no option, together with other important forms. (This is more fully described in the Counterarguments section.)

▶**Action 5:** Establish a well-diversified default investment vehicle, such as a target-date fund. Inform employees that they are free to adjust their portfolio at any time. (See Chapters 7–9 for behavioral finance tools that help employees achieve an appropriate investment strategy.)

REFERENCES

Benartzi, Shlomo, Ehud Peleg, and Richard H. Thaler. Forthcoming. "Choice Architecture and Retirement Saving Plans," in *The Behavioral Foundations of Policy*, edited by Eldar Shafir. New Jersey: Princeton University Press.

Beshears, John, James J. Choi, David Laibson, and Brigitte C. Madrian. 2009. "The Importance of Default Options for Retirement Savings Outcomes: Evidence from the United States," in Jeffrey Brown et al., eds., *Social Security Policy in a Changing Environment*. Chicago: University of Chicago Press.

———. 2010a. "The Limitations of Defaults," Prepared for the 12th Annual Joint Conference of the Retirement Research Consortium. Washington, D.C., August 5–6.

———. 2010b. "Simplification and Saving," National Bureau of Economic Research, Working Paper No. 12659.

Choi, James J., David Laibson, Brigitte C. Madrian, and Andrew Metrick. 2006. "Defined Contribution Pensions: Plan Rules, Participant Decisions, and the Path of Least Resistance," in *Tax Policy and the Economy*, vol. 16, James Poterba, ed., Cambridge: MIT Press.

GAO Report, 2009. "Retirement Savings."

Harris Interactive Inc. 2007. "Retirement Made Simpler."

Johnson, Eric J., and Daniel G. Goldstein. 2003. "Do Defaults Save Lives?" *Science* 302 (21 November): 1338–39.

Madrian, Brigitte C. 2011. Personal communication.

Madrian, Brigitte C., and Dennis F. Shea. 2001. "The Power of Suggestion: Inertia in 401(k) Participation and Savings Behavior." *The Quarterly Journal of Economics* 116, no. 4: 1149–87.

PSCA. 2010. 53rd Annual Survey.

Samuelson, William, and Richard J. Zeckhauser. 1988. "Status Quo Bias in Decision Making." *Journal of Risk and Uncertainty* 1 (March): 7–59.

CHAPTER 2

MATCH OPTIMIZER

PREVIEW

As of 2009, about 40 percent of 401(k) plans at large U.S. employers included Auto-Takeoff for new hires. Almost three-quarters of those employers whose plans are Auto-Grounded say they are reluctant to adopt Auto-Takeoff because of the prospect of the higher costs in employer-matching contributions if, as would happen, more of their employees participate (Aon Hewitt, 2011). Match Optimizer is aimed principally at these employers. It manages employers' hypersensitivity to losses by ensuring that their retirement plan costs increase only minimally, if at all, even when the adoption of Auto-Takeoff results in a large increase in plan participation. A secondary target of Match Optimizer is employers with Auto-Takeoff plans who want to utilize their match formula more effectively to help their employees save more.

Eighty percent of 401(k) plans include some degree of employer match, the most common formula being a contribution of fifty cents on the dollar on the first 6 percent of pay (PSCA, 2011). The employer match is widely assumed in the popular press and among policy makers to play an important role in boosting employee participation and saving in 401(k) plans. Researchers' conclusions on the matter over the past two decades, however, give only limited support to these assumptions.

Research on employer match has examined three issues: the existence of the match, the match rate (number of cents on the dollar), and the match cap (the percent of salary up to which the match applies). The existence of a match has been shown to have a positive, though secondary, influence on participation. By contrast, the specific match rate appears to have little or no impact on participation. Compared with the power of Auto-Takeoff, therefore, the employer match offers little leverage for significantly increasing plan participation.

The match *cap* does, however, influence how much employees are willing to save. A significant percentage of employees elects to contribute at the level of the cap. Therefore, a higher cap (within a reasonable range) will lead many people to save more.

These various lines of research offer the possibility of a behavioral intervention, the Match Optimizer, which is a novel match formula. By changing the choice architecture, the Match Optimizer allows loss-averse employers to adopt Auto-Takeoff, which will boost participation, while *not* incurring significantly higher plan costs. At the same time it has the important side benefit of many employees saving more, which is what many say they want to do.

DOES THE MATCH MATTER?

The employer match is very popular. Eighty percent of 401(k) plans include some degree of match, with the most common formula being a contribution of 50 cents on the dollar on the first 6 percent of pay (PSCA, 2011). (See Figure 2-1.) The issue here is what influence the match has on employees' participation and saving behavior. We saw in the previous chapter that studies on the effect of Auto-Takeoff on employee participation in 401(k) plans produced unequivocal answers. The answers are so clear in part because the impact is so substantial, often raising employee participation in 401(k) plans from Auto-Grounded levels of between 30 to 70 percent to between 85 to 95 percent at six months of tenure (Beshears et al., 2009a, Choi et al., 2006). The fact that researchers usually faced a relatively clear-cut test situation—going from Auto-Grounded to Auto-Takeoff within a firm—also contributed to producing a clear-cut answer. This happy state of affairs does not hold true when asking questions about the effect of the employer match on employees' saving behaviors.

Researchers seeking to determine the impact of employer match on employee saving behavior have two paths they can follow. First, they can look at the impact on saving behavior within firms that have changed some aspect of the match (introduced one where previously there was none, for example, or increased the match rate or match cap from previous levels). Second, they can compare saving behavior in employees in different companies whose match formulas differ.

The first approach, time-series studies, is preferable, because it can potentially give clearer answers than comparisons across firms. This is because, with cross-company comparisons other differences between the firms—employees' propensity to save, company culture and norms, and so on—can influence employees'

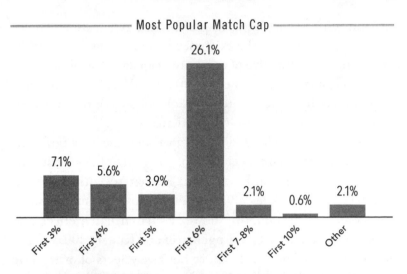

Figure 2-1. In 2010 almost half of all plans had a match of 50 cents on the dollar. The most popular match cap within that category is 6 percent of pay. (Source: data from "Matching formulas used in plans with fixed and discretionary matches" chart (pg. 29) in the 54th Annual Survey of Profit Sharing and 401(k) Plans, used with permission from Plan Sponsor Council of America.)

saving behavior regardless of the match. Nevertheless, time series studies do not guarantee clear-cut results either, because here, too, other changes might well accompany the introduction of a match or a change in match formula that may influence employees' saving behavior, again, regardless of the match.

A further compounding factor is the magnitude of the impact of various aspects of the match. If it is relatively small, as it generally seems to be, then the aforementioned "noise" in the system will often lead to ambiguous or mixed results. For the most part, this is what we see.

Almost all studies find a positive, but rather small, impact of the existence of a match on participation, in the range of 3 to 10 percentage points (Even and Macpherson, 2005). This is dwarfed by the dramatic effect of Auto-Takeoff on participation, which universally boosts participation by 15 to 25 percentage points, occasionally pushing ultimate participation close to 100 percent. Although the existence of a match nudges participation up a little, the size of the match cap has little or no effect on participation (Beshears et al., 2009b). While we encourage employers to institute a match, it is obviously not the preferred solution to the problem of low participation.

The effect of match *rate* on participation is the most problematic aspect of the employer match, in terms of research outcomes. Gary Engelhardt and Anil Kumar recently reviewed seven such studies. They found that two showed a small positive impact on participation, two showed a small negative effect, and three found no effect at all (Engelhardt and Kumar, 2003). Their own study shows one of the more positive effects of match rate on participation (Engelhardt and Kumar, 2006). They calculate from their model that in order to achieve the same impact on participation as that provided by Auto-Takeoff, employers would need to increase their current match by one dollar for every dollar contributed by employees. This would be a very expensive solution to the participation problem, and, given the efficacy and much lower cost of Auto-Takeoff, it makes no sense to go in that direction.

The one aspect of employer match that yields unambiguous and useful results is the effect of match cap on saving rates. In the absence of a match, plan participants apparently use a simple mental rule of thumb, or heuristic, to select their contribution rate: go for a round number. Under these circumstances, we see contribution rates clustering at 5, 10, and 15 percent. In the presence of a match, another heuristic comes into play: go for the match cap. For instance, one company introduced an employer match in October 2000, with a cap of 4 percent. Prior to that date, the distribution of employee contributions showed a strong round number effect. Six months after the change almost 30 percent of new plan participants chose 4 percent as their savings rate, although the round number effect was still apparent (Choi et al., 2006). In other words, the match cap has a significant impact on how much plan participants choose to save. This offers potential leverage for encouraging people to save more. (See Figure 2-2.)

The answer to this section's question, therefore, is: 1) the existence of a match doesn't matter anywhere near as much as Auto-Takeoff in promoting employee participation; 2) the match rate has little impact on employees' behavior; and 3) the match cap matters if the goal is to increase how much employees will save.

— Contribution Rates Before and After Implementing a 4% Match Cap —

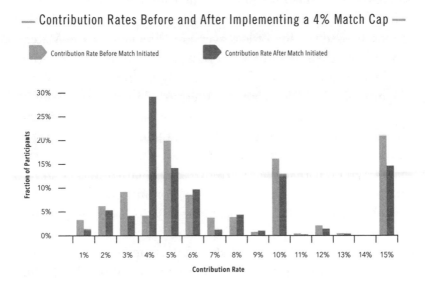

Figure 2-2. When this company introduced a match cap of 4 percent of pay where previously there was none, a significant proportion of participants shifted their saving rate to that of the cap. The round-number effect still holds, with deferral rates of 5, 10, and 15 percent being more popular than other rates, apart from the match cap. (Source: Adapted from Choi et al., 2006; data have been normalized to exclude non-participants. Poterba, James M., ed., *Tax Policy and the Economy*, Volume 16, Table 7 from article "Defined Contribution Pensions," © 2002 Massachusetts Institute of Technology, by permission of The MIT Press.)

OPTIMIZING THE MATCH

Many employers genuinely feel obligated to do the right thing for their employees, which would mean adopting Auto-Takeoff and having an employer match. However, employers are understandably hypersensitive to any increase in plan costs, and especially so in difficult economic times. Although this isn't loss aversion in the academic sense, when plan sponsors express their concerns about such increases, it *feels* like loss aversion. It feels as if they are hypersensitive to negative deviations from how much they are currently spending on the match. Employers are therefore very sensitive to even small increases in the match, which mentally they categorize as a loss, even though it is only a loosely used version of loss aversion. The goal of the Match Optimizer, then, is to find the right choice architecture—the optimal match formula—that not only addresses employers' hypersensitivity to loss, but the interests of employees as well.

From the employees' point of view, the Match Optimizer also helps people do what they say they want to do. As we saw in the Introduction, one survey found that two-thirds of plan participants admitted that they were not saving enough. The great majority of this group said they were committed to increasing their saving rate "within the next four months." As it turned out, words spoke louder than actions, and only 14 percent raised their saving rate (Choi et al., 2006). "[R]espondents overwhelmingly do not follow through on their good intentions," note the authors. Clearly, many participants could use some help in boosting their saving rate, and a 2007 Harris Interactive poll reports that an overwhelming majority of employees welcome their employer's help in saving for retirement. The Match Optimizer is a tool for offering that help.

Assume we have an Auto-Grounded 401(k) plan and a match formula of fifty cents on the dollar on the first 6 percent of pay;

and assume a participation rate of 70 percent at three years of
tenure (Choi et al., 2006). Under this formula the employer is paying 2.1 percent (50 percent match rate x 6 percent match cap x 70
percent participation) of payroll in employer matching contributions. The employer wants to adopt Auto-Takeoff but is concerned,
because of hypersensitivity to losses, about substantially increased
plan costs that would be incurred with significantly higher participation. What options are open to the choice architect?

We know that reducing the match rate has a small impact on
participation compared with Auto-Takeoff, so this is where our
leverage is. We are therefore proposing that the employer
accompanies the adoption of Auto-Takeoff with some change in
the match formula, including reducing the match rate, designed
to keep down the employer's plan costs. What are the options
employers might want to (or should) consider?

Option 1: change the formula to
25 cents up to 6 percent of pay.

Under Auto-Takeoff, we can assume that participation will rise
20+ percent to, say, 90 percent. The employer would now be
contributing a total of 1.35 percent (25 percent match x 6 percent
cap x 90 percent participation) of payroll in matching funds
under this match formula. The employer would no doubt be
happy, because he is now spending considerably less (1.35 percent of payroll versus 2.1 percent) than previously. The employees, however, would have every reason to be unhappy because,
although more of them would be participating where previously
they weren't, existing plan members would now be receiving
only half as much in employer match as they did previously. And
they would be saving a total of 7.5 percent of pay (employee and
employer contributions combined) compared with 9 percent
under the previous formula. Although under this formula those

20 percent of employees who are now saving (where previously they were not) will benefit from this formula, those employees who were already on the plan will receive less in employer matching contributions. The employer will, of course, be spending less in matching contributions. This is obviously not optimal and we do not recommend it.

Option 2: change the formula to 25 cents up to 10 percent of pay.

Again assume a participation rate of 90 percent after adopting Auto-Takeoff. In the extreme case in which all participants are saving at the cap of 10 percent, the employer would be contributing 2.25 percent (25 percent match x 10 percent cap x 90 percent participation) of payroll in matching funds. This would represent a slight increase (0.15 percent of payroll) compared to the original formula. However, experience shows that although saving to the cap is a popular rule of thumb, it is by no means the universal choice; in which case, under this new optimized match, the employer might not see his contributions rise much at all.

Those employees who do contribute up to the cap would now be saving appreciably more than under the original plan. Under the original match formula of fifty cents on the dollar up to 6 percent of pay, employees who contribute up to the cap would be saving a total of 9 percent (employee and employer contribution combined). Under the optimized match formula of twenty-five cents on the dollar up to 10 percent of pay, employees contributing to the cap would save 10 percent of their pay, which would be matched by a further 2.5 percent from the employer, giving a total of 12.5 percent. This amounts to a savings increase of close to 40 percent. As noted above, most people say they would like to save more (Choi et al., 2006), and the Match Optimizer is a behavioral path to help them do that.

We strongly recommend this optimized formula, for three reasons. First, although the employer's plan costs might rise slightly, he will have the satisfaction of knowing that more of his employees are participating, which many employers say they want (Deloitte, 2010). Second, many employees are saving more, which, as mentioned, is what they say they want. Third, people have a very strong sense of what is fair and what is not (Kahneman et al., 1986). In this case, with proper communication, employees will likely recognize the fairness involved when the employer spends a little more on total matching contributions, even though some individual plan participants might receive less in employer match.

For the employer who is struggling financially and wants to adopt Auto-Takeoff without incurring any extra costs, we offer option three.

Option 3: change the formula to 20 cents up to 10 percent of pay.

The bottom line for the employer in this case is that he is contributing 1.8 percent (20 percent match x 10 percent cap x 90 percent participation) of payroll in matching funds. He no doubt would be happy to be now paying out less than under the original, Auto-Grounded Plan. From the employees' point of view, under this plan formula many would be saving 12 percent of pay (employee and employer contributions combined). This is a little less than under option two, but still better than under the original match formula.

Figure 2-3 gives an overview of the different options presented here, showing the impact on likely employee deferral and the cost of each option to the employer.

The choice of a 10 percent match cap in the above options is quite deliberate, for two reasons. First, it enables people to save

——————————— Outcomes of Different Match Formulas ———————————

	The Formula	Likely Employee Deferral*	Combined Employee/Employer Deferral	Employer Cost (% of Payroll)
Status Quo	50¢ up to 6%	6.0%	9.0%	2.10%
Option 1	25¢ up to 6%	6.0%	7.5%	1.35%
Option 2	25¢ up to 10%	10.0%	12.5%	2.25%
Option 3	20¢ up to 10%	10.0%	12.0%	1.80%

*Assuming employees save to the cap

Figure 2–3.

significantly more. And second, it plays into the round-number effect. We saw earlier that people's contributions cluster around the cap, and that they also like round numbers: 5, 10, and 15 percent. In the example of the company earlier that adopted a match with a cap of 4 percent, a 4 percent contribution was subsequently by far the most popular saving rate, but many people still saved at 5, 10, and 15 percent. Choosing a cap of 10 percent therefore doubles up on the two behavioral tendencies: saving to the cap, and the round-number effect. This would represent a bold departure from industry practice, as fewer than 1 percent of existing plans currently match up to 10 percent (PSCA, 2011). (See Figure 2–1.)

If the new, optimized match formula is adopted, we recommend that the employer develops a communication plan designed to convey its motivations to employees:

- We (the employer) are motivated to help more employees participate in a retirement plan, by adopting Auto-Takeoff.

- We are also motivated to help employees save more in the plan than they are already doing, by raising the match cap, to ensure a financially secure retirement future.
- In order to achieve these goals aimed at benefitting employees, the company will be paying more in overall matching contributions, which it considers a worthwhile tradeoff for those benefits.

However the communication plan is carried out, the goal should be to give employees the information they need to understand the proposed change, and to respond to their questions.

Although the Match Optimizer is aimed principally at helping employers dramatically increase participation by adopting Auto-Takeoff (while also managing their hypersensitivity to loss), it is also relevant to employers with plans that already have Auto-Takeoff. If the existing match formula is fifty cents on the dollar up to the first 6 percent of pay, the employer could optimize the match formula to thirty cents up to 10 percent of pay. He could then tell his employees that he is making the change to encourage people to save more, while the company is actually spending the same in matching contributions.

COUNTERARGUMENTS

The Match Optimizer violates all three safe-harbor employer contribution requirements.

On its face, that is correct, though currently two-thirds of plans do not use the safe-harbor provisions (PSCA 2011). For the one-third of plans that do choose safe harbor by design, here is what they can do to have a strong likelihood of passing the non-discrimination test without the safe-harbor provisions and benefit from the Match Optimizer.

The Average Deferral Percentage (ADP) rules of the non-discrimination test require the following, in which the percentages in the left hand column are averages for eligible employees (whether or not they are deferring):

──────────── Non-Discrimination Test Requirements ────────────

If Lower-Income Employees Defer:	Higher-Income Employees Cannot Defer More Than:
0 – 2 percent	2 times more
2 – 8 percent	2 percent more
Over 8 percent	1.25 times more

Figure 2–4.

There are two elements to the optimized match that will enable the plan to pass the non-discrimination test: 1) the Auto-Takeoff feature; 2) the recommended match cap of 10 percent.

Although we often speak of Auto-Takeoff as raising plan participation from 70 to 90 percent, these necessarily are averages. The key fact about Auto-Takeoff here is that it has a disproportionate effect on participation with lower-income employees. In one study, 13 percent of lower-income employees joined a plan under Auto-Grounded, as compared with 68 percent for higher-income employees, a disparity of 55 percentage points. When Auto-Takeoff was introduced, the disparity shrank dramatically to 14 percentage points (80 percent versus 94 percent). (Madrian and Shea, 2001.)

We can assume, then, that when Auto-Takeoff is introduced under the Match Optimizer program, 80 percent of lower-income employees will participate in the plan. In the previous chapter we recommend that employees have a default saving rate of 6 percent under Auto-Takeoff. Because of inertia, many will not change it. In Chapters 4 and 5 we will describe behavioral interventions that help participants raise their saving rate to 10 percent within two years of enrollment. Within a short time of adopting Auto-Takeoff and the Match Optimizer, therefore, most plan participants will be saving at 10 percent. The average saving rate of lower-income employees (including the 20 percent who contribute zero) is therefore close to 8 percent (10 x 0.8). According to the ADP test above, this means that higher-income employees can contribute 10 percent (1.25 x 8) on average. Now, we can expect participation in this cohort to be around 94 percent, which allows those who do participate to contribute around 10.5 percent on average. With an employer match such as we recommend for an optimized match formula, the total savings rate rises to 13 percent. So, unless a high proportion of highly paid employees are deferring more than the respectable rate of 10 percent, the plan will easily pass the non-discrimination testing.

Notice that the typical Auto-Takeoff default saving rate of 3 percent will not provide protection against the non-discrimination test, because the higher-income employees would be limited to saving no more than approximately 5 percent, which most in that group would find unacceptable.

Existing plan participants will object to the new match formula, because they will be receiving less in employer match.

There may well be some employees who are concerned primarily with their own interests. But we believe that when the motivation for a new match formula is carefully explained as a way of helping more of their workmates— especially the younger, lower-income, less educated—and themselves save for their retirement, many will see the benefit and will appreciate that the company is acting for the greater good. It will appeal to their innate sense of fairness.

BEHAVIORAL FINANCE ACTIONS

▶**Action 1:** Develop an appropriate communication program to explain the motives behind the introduction of an optimized match formula and to respond to employees' questions.

▶**Action 2:** Adopt Auto-Takeoff and optimize the plan's match formula to something like option 2 on page 66. For example, if the match formula used to be fifty cents on the dollar up to the first 6 percent of pay, then reformulate it to twenty-five cents on the dollar up to the first 10 percent of pay.

▶**Action 3:** If the employer's 401(k) plan already has an Auto-Takeoff feature, he should consider increasing the match cap to 10 percent while reducing the match rate from its current level so that employees receive the same contribution from the employer and his costs stay the same (going from fifty cents on the dollar up to 6 percent of pay, to thirty cents on the dollar up to 10 percent of pay, for example). Under this optimized formula, and with behavioral interventions described in Chapters 4 and 5, many employees will save up to the optimized cap and will therefore save more.

REFERENCES

Aon Hewitt. 2011. "Hot Topics in Retirement: A Changing Horizon."

Beshears, John, James J. Choi, David Laibson, and Brigitte C. Madrian. 2009a. "The Importance of Default Options for Retirement Savings Outcomes: Evidence from the United States." In Jeffrey Brown et al., eds., *Social Security Policy in a Changing Environment*. Chicago: University of Chicago Press.

———. 2009b. "The Impact of Employer Matching on Savings Plan Participation under Automatic Enrollment." In *Research Findings in the Economics of Aging*, edited by D. A. Wise. Chicago: University of Chicago Press.

Choi, James J., David Laibson, Brigitte C. Madrian, and Andrew Metrick. 2006. "Saving for Retirement on the Path of Least Resistance." In *Behavioral Public Finance: Toward a New Agenda*, edited by Edward J. McCaffrey and Joel Slemrod. New York: Russell Sage Foundation, 304–51.

Deloitte. 2010. *401(k) Benchmarking Survey*.

Engelhardt, Gary V., and Anil Kumar. 2003. "Understanding the Impact of Employer Matching on 401(k) Saving." *Research Dialogue* (TIAA-CREF Institute) no. 76 (June).

———. 2006. "Employer Matching and 401(k) Saving: Evidence from the Health and Retirement Study." Working Paper 12447, National Bureau of Economic Research.

Even, William E., and David A. Macpherson. 2005. "The Effects of Employer Matching in 401(k) Plans." *Industrial Relations* 44: 525–49.

Harris Interactive. 2007. "Retirement Made Simpler."

Kahneman, Daniel, Jack L. Knetch, and Richard H. Thaler. 1986. "Fairness and the Assumptions of Economics." *The Journal of Business* 59, no. 4: S285–S300.

Madrian, Brigitte C., and Dennis F. Shea. 2001. "The Power of Suggestion: Inertia in 401(k) Participation and Savings Behavior." *The Quarterly Journal of Economics* 116, no. 4: 1149–87.

PSCA, 2011. "54th Annual Survey."

CHAPTER 3

THE FACE TOOL

PREVIEW

Economists have long been aware of the human weakness for immediate gratification: we know what we want, and we want it *now!*—even if it isn't a matter of genuine urgency. We find it very difficult to delay pleasure in favor of some benefit in the future, a fact that the English economist Nassau William Senior noted more than a century and a half ago: "To abstain from the enjoyment which is in our power, or to seek distant rather than immediate results, are among the most painful exertions of the human will." (Senior, 1836.) Most of us have experienced this pain at some time or other.

Senior is describing the behavioral challenge we call myopia, or, more specifically here, temporal myopia. Just as Mr. Magoo's visual myopia renders him unable to see clearly even over a short distance, as we saw in the Introduction, we temporal myopics find it hard to bring into mental focus the importance of situations or actions in our distant future. This myopia contributes to many peoples' failure to enroll in a retirement plan.

Two factors are at play here. One is our strong tendency to place greater value on *lifestyle experience* in the present than we do on greater rewards in the future. We will explore this issue of temporal discounting, and present a behavioral solution that circumvents it, in Chapter 6. The second factor is our perception of *self*, specifically, our perception of present self in relation to our future self, and how this impacts our willingness to save for our retirement. This is the topic for the current chapter.

Psychologists have known for a long time that young people do not readily identify with their own future selves, for example, a thirty-year-old thinking about someone at the age of sixty-five and entering retirement. In the extreme, that future self can seem like a stranger, someone for whom we would be unwilling to make sacrifices now. This is called the *identity gap*. At the same time, people place much more weight on emotions they experience in the present than on emotions they are able to imagine their older selves feeling. This is an *empathy gap*.

In this chapter we present a behavioral intervention based on digital age-progression and morphing technology that enables people to see their future selves and witness emotions in their future selves, thus closing the identity and empathy gaps. This experience makes people more willing to say they will begin saving for their retirement.

YOUR TWO SELVES

Think about this for a moment. You are yourself today; of that you can be certain. What about ten years from now? Thirty years from now? Who will that future person be? It is still you, of course, but is it the same "self"? The issue of the "continuity of self" has been a long-standing puzzle to philosophers, from the ancient Greeks onwards. And, as we will see here, it has a practical dimension, too, in people's willingness to prepare for their retirement.

The key issue here is this: does your future self *feel* like your present self? How psychologically connected are you—are we all—to our future selves? There is now much evidence from psychology and neurobiology that the answer to the latter question is, "Not very." In the extreme, as we said, that future self can seem like a stranger to us. The eighteenth-century English philosopher Joseph Butler recognized this, and set out the inevitable conclusion in an essay he wrote in 1736: "If the self or person of today, and that of tomorrow, are not the same, but only like persons, the person of today is really no more interested in what will befall the person of tomorrow, than in what will befall any other person."

Two and a half centuries later, another English philosopher, Derek Parfit, expanded on this idea. "Reconsider a boy who starts to smoke, knowing and hardly caring that this may cause him to suffer greatly fifty years later," he wrote in 1987. "This boy does not identify with his future self. His attitude towards his future self is in some ways like his attitude to other people." Parfit had earlier attributed this psychological disconnection to "a failure of imagination" (Parfit, 1971). It is, in effect, a failure to *identify* with one's future self. As a consequence, the idea of setting aside a portion of one's current salary to be deposited in a retirement account can seem like making sacrifices now in order to give money to a stranger in the future. Who would want to do that? In any case, retirement seems like a distant prospect to young people, so it is very easy for them to say, "I'll get around to it later, when it really matters."

With the benefit of neuroimaging, it is now possible to see with one's own eyes what previously were merely philosophical musings, interesting though they were. Neuroimaging shows us graphically why the decision to save for retirement is so hard. Hal Hershfield, currently of New York University, along with various colleagues, uses functional magnetic resonance imaging (fMRI) to reveal patterns of brain activity when the topic under consideration is self versus a stranger. In some instances, fMRI can give a more objective insight into a person's thought process than can be elicited by asking them questions.

For instance, when someone is asked to think about himself or herself, fMRI detects a particular pattern of brain activity in the mid-front section of the cerebral cortex. We will call this Pattern A. Next, when that person is asked to think about a stranger, a different pattern of activity takes place in this same area. We will call this Pattern B. The question Hershfield and his colleagues then asked was: what pattern of brain activity do you see when this same person thinks about his or her future self? Is it more like A, the "self" pattern? Or more like B, the "stranger" pattern? The answer is unequivocal. It is more like B. In other words, when we think about our future self, our brain treats this as if we were thinking about a stranger (Ersner-Hershfield et al., 2009a; Hershfield, 2011a). No doubt Joseph Butler would have approved this twenty-first-century confirmation of his eighteenth-century musings.

A group of eighteen young men and women went through this procedure and, not surprisingly, the results varied somewhat. The brains of some subjects lit up the Pattern B (stranger) activity signature more strongly than others when thinking about their own future selves. And this is where the research becomes really interesting, and extremely pertinent. A week after they had gone through neuroimaging, the subjects went back to the lab and did a temporal-discounting task. This involved electing whether to receive a certain sum of money now, or a larger sum at some specified time in the future. Once again, the subjects varied in their propensity for temporal discounting: some were impatient, and said they wanted to take the money now; others were more patient, and opted to wait.

The importance of this study is in how these two measures—brain activity pattern and degree of temporal discounting—correlate. The data show that those people whose brains had a strong "stranger" activity signature when thinking about their future selves were the impatient ones on the temporal-discounting test. Put another way, people who are less connected to their future selves are more myopic, and prefer immediate gratification over waiting for a greater benefit in the future.

These temporal-discounting tests were done in the laboratory. But there is also a link in the real world between people's sense of identity with their future selves and their ability to delay immediate gratification by saving, as revealed by a second, parallel study. Here, 164 Stanford undergraduates were asked to say how much they identified with their future self, using the Future Self-Continuity Scale. This study involves choosing which pair of overlapping circles (representing current and future selves) best represented their feelings (Ersner-Hershfield et al., 2009b). The bigger the overlap, the closer the sense of identity, and vice versa.

Once again, some people felt more connected to their future selves than others did. And once again, those subjects who confessed to feeling less connected were most impatient on a laboratory-conducted temporal-discounting test similar to the one described previously. At the same time, a group of 155 adult subjects (with an average age a little over fifty) disclosed their total financial worth (assets minus liabilities), after completing the Future Self-Continuity Scale. Bottom line: those people who feel more connected to their future selves had greater financial worth than those who identified less closely with their future selves (Ersner-Hershfield et al., 2009b).

These are very significant findings because they link people's thoughts and emotions to financial decisions in a more direct way than is usually possible to ascertain in economics. In the conclusion to their paper, the authors write: "Enhancing future self-continuity might encourage people to save for the future." That is our goal here.

VIRTUAL WORLDS

We are here entering a world that just a few years ago would have seemed like science fiction, but is now "science fact." It is a virtual world in which people can see highly realistic, digitized versions of themselves, morphed in some predetermined way. And when people observe their avatars, or digital self-images, they are often profoundly influenced by the avatars' behavior. For instance, imagine you were to watch as your avatar resolutely exercised in a gym, losing weight as a result. What would you do? If you are like most people, next time you get on your exercise bike or go for a run, you would apply yourself to the task with more dedication than previously.

Now imagine your avatar at a cocktail party, elegantly turned out, perhaps a few inches trimmer around the waist, a few inches taller, and most definitely more charming and witty than your real self. What now? Next time you are in a similar social situation you will most likely carry yourself with more confidence and more self-assurance, and you will definitely be wittier.

These new versions of yourself—the person who exercises more vigorously and the person who cuts a more striking presence at a party—are not the result of your actively trying harder to change. The new you emerges without effort, born unconsciously as a result of having "been" that new you in a virtual world. Nick Yee and Jeremy Bailenson, virtual-reality researchers at Stanford, have named this the "Proteus* Effect" (Yee and Bailenson, 2007). Bailenson explains it this way: "You already know that your physical appearance affects your attitudes, your emotions, and your behavior even if you are not consciously thinking about it. The same thing happens in virtual reality, when you become this person with a different body or face. Those features of your avatar affect your mind" (Zweig, 2011). They affect your mind when you are your avatar in the virtual world and, more significantly, they affect your mind when you return to your real self in the real world (Blascovich and Bailenson, 2011).

When he was at Stanford, in Bailenson's virtual-reality lab, Hershfield recognized that there was a way to close the identity gap and the empathy gap and thereby perhaps lead people to be more willing to save for their future selves. Through the magical quality of virtual reality, showing people their future selves makes concrete the fact that the person who will be embarking on retirement in thirty years' time is connected to the present self. By doing so, we might then be able to answer in the affirmative the poignant question in Paul McCartney's song: "Will you still feed me, when I'm sixty-four?"

"Why resort to fancy technology," you might say, "when you can simply ask people to think about themselves at sixty-five and imagine how their future selves might feel about their new stage

---

* Proteus was an early sea god of Greek mythology who was able to change shape when it suited him; hence *protean*, possessing a versatile nature.

of life?" It's a good question. But it turns out that people find it extremely challenging to perform that apparently simple task, for several reasons. For a start, it's not something that we routinely do, so that thought path is foreign cognitive territory for most of us. In addition, imagining oneself thirty years in the future conjures up many different contingencies and images—such as losing one's hair, winning the lottery, moving to another town or country, having a facelift, meeting the person of one's dreams—which leads to multiple (and different) future selves. Faced with this spate of possible future selves, people find it very hard to bring into focus a single, salient future self. With a nod to L. P. Hartley, we could say: The future is a foreign country; they do things differently there. We need help to grasp the reality of that foreign country, and virtual reality is a promising approach.

That help comes from the project that Hershfield initiated while he was at Stanford, and now lists six co-authors, including Bailenson, Dan Goldstein of the London Business School, and William F. Sharpe, the Nobel Prize–winning economist and co-founder of Financial Engines (Hershfield et al., 2011).

The first phase of the project involves immersive virtual-reality environments, with Stanford undergraduates as subjects. Subjects wear a headset through which they see the virtual world. They enter a small room that is empty except for half a dozen cameras that closely monitor the subjects' every movement. The information is fed into a high-powered "rendering" computer, which sends a digitized version of the participant—his or her avatar—to the visor on the headset. In a virtual mirror on the virtual wall, the participants see the avatars moving about the room, just as they themselves are moving.

Subjects are in two groups. One group sees avatars of their current selves, while the other sees age-progressed avatars of their future selves. The age progression is based on photographs of the subjects, and is produced by a software package, in three stages: 1) It locates key points on the facial anatomy from front-on and profile photographs; 2) builds a three-dimensional model of the face; and 3) morphs the shape and texture of the model to create a realistic rendering of the participant at age seventy. The hair color is changed to gray using Adobe Photoshop.

The aged avatars are very convincing, and elicit such reactions as: "Wow, I look just like Grandma," "Oooh, I don't know if I want to see this," and "Whoa, this is freaky!" (Hershfield, 2011b). The experimenters were careful not to produce aged avatars that might be described as "gross." An image of that sort was thought possibly to have the opposite of the desired result in that it might widen, not narrow, the identity gap between a participant's present and future self.

The second part of the study involved subjects performing a simple money-allocation task, created specifically for this experiment. Subjects were told they had unexpectedly received $1,000 and were asked how they might plan to use it, with the following options: 1) to buy something nice for a special person; 2) to invest in a retirement account; 3) to plan a fun and extravagant occasion; or 4) to put into a checking account.

There is a difference between *knowing* on an intellectual level that one will be old at some point in the future and *feeling* it on an emotional level. The researchers expected that "making one's acquaintance" with one's future self would be a step toward engendering that feeling. They predicted that the virtual-reality experience would help subjects connect with their future selves, close the identity and empathy gaps, and be more willing to save for retirement. That is exactly what happened. Subjects who experienced their future selves said they would allot more than twice as much to the hypothetical retirement account ($172) compared with those who saw a digitized version of their current selves ($80). Subjects did not increase their willingness to save when they saw aged avatars of other people, so this is not simply a "priming effect," or bringing to mind the idea of being old.

Intuitively, one might expect a gender difference in subjects' responses to seeing their aged future selves. However, the experimenters saw no difference between men and women in their responses to seeing their aged future selves. There remains the possibility, of course, that gender differences might arise in older age groups.

This was the first demonstration of a novel kind of intervention that encourages people to make good financial decisions about their retirement future through closing the identity gap between one's own present and future selves.

THE FACE TOOL

Building on promising results, Hershfield, Goldstein, and Sharpe undertook a fascinating study with two important new elements. One was to replace the temporal discounting task with a more relevant financial decision, namely, what proportion of salary subjects would be willing to set aside for a retirement account after experiencing their future selves. The second was to emotionally engage the subjects more directly by having the digitized present self and future self faces display feelings in response to the realities of saving behavior. For instance, a high saving rate would cause the present self to look sad, while the future self would be smiling. Similarly, a low saving rate would cause the present self to look happy while the future self would frown with displeasure or unhappiness.

Subjects provided three photographs of themselves: a happy face, a neutral face, and a sad face. These formed the basis of a software-generated continuum of about a dozen faces, ranging in mood from very sad to very happy, for both the current self and the age-morphed future self. This "sliding scale" of emotions was linked to a sliding scale of allocation of pay to retirement savings, from zero on the left to a maximum (say, 20 percent) on the right. Built into the system were various factors,

---------------- The Impact of Seeing Your Future Self ----------------

Seeing our future selves boosts savings

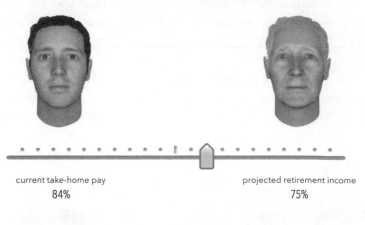

current take-home pay   projected retirement income
84%   75%

Seeing a happy future self further boosts savings

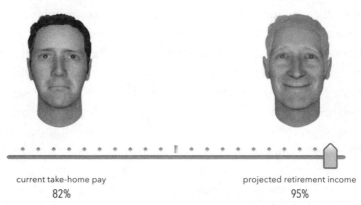

current take-home pay   projected retirement income
82%   95%

Figure 3-1. Experiments with digital age-morphing technology show that when subjects see future renditions of themselves they are prepared to save more for their retirement. Similarly, a happy-looking future self is associated with increased savings. (Source: Allianz Global Investors White Paper, *Behavioral Finance in Action*, with illustrations based on the work of Hal Hershfield and his coworkers.)

such as age at starting to work (twenty-three), retirement age (sixty-eight), and a salary of $64,000 (in today's dollars) by age forty. Displayed on the slider was current take-home pay on the left, and projected future retirement income on the right, both of which changed in response to the position of the slider. As the slider was moved toward the left, the present self looked ever happier (thinking of all those treats he or she would be able to buy), while the future self looked ever sadder (contemplating a deprived retirement). And when the slider was moved toward the right, indicating a higher deferral of pay to retirement savings, the future self beamed while the present self was less than happy. (See Figure 3-1.)

Subjects in the study, who once again were Stanford students, carried out the procedure online, half seeing digitized renditions of their current self, the other half seeing their future self. They were free to move the slider as they wished, and could see the result in changes in current take-home pay and projected future retirement income, as well as the changes in facial expression. Once again there was a marked difference in people's willingness to save, depending on which version of themselves they saw. In this case, subjects who saw their future self elected to save 30 percent more in their hypothetical retirement fund than those who had seen their current self (6.76 percent as compared with 5.20 percent). Such a difference would have a significant impact on the total savings accumulated over a period of, say, thirty years (Hershfield et al., 2011).*

The researchers believe that the response is the result of closing the identity and empathy gaps, and they actually took steps to measure that by using the Future Self-Continuity Scale mentioned earlier. Subjects who had seen their future self scored 35 percent higher on this test (4.39 as against 3.25, on a seven-point

---

* A second study on eighteen- to thirty-year-old men and women showed that this was not simply a response to happy or sad expressions. Essentially the same result was obtained when the facial expression remained neutral, no matter where the slider was.

scale, where seven is very strong Future Self-Continuity), indicating that the procedure really does shift people's connection with their future selves. This correlates well with savings decisions, as we would predict.

Research shows that people are much more likely to face up to psychologically tough decisions when they are engaged in a fun and entertaining way (Laran and Janiszewski, in press). This innovative idea of experiencing one's future self certainly qualifies as bringing to mind decisions about retirement in a more compelling way than many conventional tools, such as the avalanche of online calculators full of numbers and tables. The behavioral intervention is effective because it engages people's emotions, whereas the conventional educational approach typically does not. And the pace at which this area of virtual-worlds technology is developing is accelerating. "The notion of people interacting via avatars with their bank accounts or financial planners is not an outlandish one," note Hershfield and his coauthors.

We are calling this approach the Behavioral Time Machine concept, to which we will return in Chapters 6 and 9. It is about different ways of connecting the present self to future selves in different domains. In this chapter the realm is of the experience of future self as *self*, in Chapter 6 it is the experience of future *lifestyle*, and in Chapter 9 it affords a glimpse of one's future *financial reality*. The technology that facilitates connection with one's own future self described above is called the Face Tool, and different categories of users will interface with it in different ways. This includes financial advisers working with individuals on saving and wealth management, and financial advisers helping employers structure their 401(k) plan. The Face Tool is designed to solve the problem of a lack of identification with one's future self, with the result that people will be more willing to save for their retirement.

We are in the process of transforming the Face Tool technology to a scale that is practical in the 401(k) world. The ultimate goal is to have the entire process integrated with 401(k) record-keeping systems.* During the enrollment process, eligible employees will be invited to upload their photo (or have the tool automatically import a photo from the employer's files). They will then be able to observe their future self respond emotionally to different levels of present saving rates, just as the subjects in the experiments did. Making the acquaintance of one's future self would therefore be easy. We know from the above experiments that such an experience will make employees more willing to save. We also know from other researchers' observations that good intentions are rarely carried through, unless acted upon immediately (Choi et al., 2006). Employees' experience with the Face Tool should therefore be tied closely to the decision to save, on the spot.

COUNTERARGUMENTS

You have described experimental studies, not real-life tests. How do you know the study will do what you expect in the real world?

That is a very good point, and it echoes an observation made recently by economists Steven D. Levitt and John A. List: "Perhaps the greatest challenge facing behavioral economics is demonstrating its applicability in the real world" (Levitt and List, 2008). While it is true that all of the psychological factors that we hold to be important in behavioral finance research were initially identified in the laboratory, we

---

* A stand-alone version will also be available for financial advisers working with individual clients on saving and wealth management issues.

contend that they are readily apparent in people's judgments and decisions in the real world of finance. Skeptics might, however, demand a scientifically verified demonstration of such behaviors in the real world. We offer one here, in the world of professional golf. Economists Devin Pope and Maurice Schweitzer analyzed more than 2.5 million putts by professional golfers on the PGA Tour, using precise laser measurements. They found a clear demonstration of loss aversion in the way top golfers approach two different kinds of shots (Pope and Schweitzer, 2011).

Many people will find this story hard to believe, but it is true. In golf tournaments it is a player's *total* score at the end of eighteen holes (a round) that counts, which implies that they should focus equally as hard for each and every shot during the round. But it turns out that these best-of-the-best professionals put just a little bit extra psychological effort into a certain kind of shot compared with others. Pope and Schweitzer studied two kinds of shots of comparable length and circumstances, one that would result in a birdie (one under par) and the other that would result in par. "Par" is the typical number of shots a professional golfer should take to complete a particular hole.

Sinking either a birdie or a par shot gives the same numerical result: one shot, so there should be no difference in the success rates of these two shots. But there is a difference, small but statistically robust. Pope and Schweitzer found that top professionals are 2 to 4 percentage points more likely to sink a par shot than a birdie of equal length. They explain the difference in the following way. Failing to sink a birdie is regrettable, because it represents a missed opportunity to improve the player's total score, and this can be thought of as a foregone gain. Failing to sink a par shot would be seriously painful for a professional golfer's pride, because he or she should expect to achieve par at every hole, and not doing so is perceived as a loss. Because of loss aversion, a loss is more painful than a foregone gain. Professionals therefore put more effort into par shots, in an attempt to avoid the pain of that loss. The difference—2 to 4 percentage points—might not seem like much, but it is worth potentially millions of dollars to professionals on the PGA Tour. "In short," say Pope and Schweitzer, "our findings demonstrate that loss aversion persists in a market setting with intense competition, large stakes, and very experienced agents."

This is a very striking example of a behavioral principle that was identified in "thought experiments" in the lab and then applied to real-life experience. Will what we've seen in the lab with the Face Tool also translate just as well to real life? Obviously, we cannot guarantee that it will, but even if it works only half as well in the field as it does in the lab, that still represents a significant improvement in saving behavior.

BEHAVIORAL FINANCE ACTIONS

▶ **Action 1:** Encourage your record keeper to have the Face Tool feature available to employees. During the enrollment process, invite eligible employees to upload their photo (or have it automatically import a photo from your files). They will then be able to observe their future self responding emotionally to different levels of present saving rates, just as the subjects in the experiments did. As a result, they should be more willing to enroll in the company's retirement plan.

▶ **Action 2:** Ensure that employees' Face Tool experience is integrated with their decision to save, on the spot.

▶ **Action 3:** The behavioral finance capability of record keepers is important in enabling them to establish behaviorally healthy plans, with high participation, adequate saving, and wise asset allocation. Your choice of a record keeper should therefore be influenced by his capability in this area of expertise.

REFERENCES

Blascovich, Jim, and Jeremy N. Bailenson. 2011. *Infinite Reality*. New York: William Morrow.

Choi, James J., David Laibson, Brigitte C. Madrian, and Andrew Metrick. 2006. "Defined Contribution Pensions: Plan Rules, Participant Decisions, and the Path of Least Resistance." In *Tax Policy and the Economy*, vol. 16, edited by James Poterba. Cambridge: MIT Press.

Ersner-Hershfield, Hal, G. Elliott Wimmer, and Brian Knutson. 2009a. "Saving for the Future Self: Neural Measures of the Future Self-continuity Predict Temporal Discounting." *SCAN* 4: 85–92.

Ersner-Hershfield, Hal, M. Tess Garton, Kacey Ballard, Gregory R. Samanez-Larkin, and Brian Knutson. 2009b. "Don't Stop Thinking about Tomorrow: Individual Differences in Future Self-continuity Account for Saving." *Judgment and Decision Making* 4, no. 4: 280–86.

Hershfield, Hal. 2011. 2011. "Future Self-continuity: How Conceptions of the Future Self Transform Intertemporal Choice." *Annals of the New York Academy of Science* 1,235: 30–45.

———. Personal communication.

Hershfield, Hal, Daniel G. Goldstein, William F. Sharpe, Jesse Fox, Leo Yeykelis, Laura L. Carstensen, and Jeremy N. Bailenson. 2011. "Increasing Saving Behavior through Age-progressed Renderings of the Future Self." Special issue, *Journal of Marketing Research* 48: S23–S37.

Laran, Juliano, and Chris Janiszewski. Forthcoming. "Work or Fun? How Task Construal and Completion Influence Regulatory Behavior." *Journal of Consumer Research*

Levitt, Steven D., and John A. List. 2008. "Homo Economicus Evolves." *Science* 319: 909–10.

Parfit, Derek. 1971. "Personal Identity." *Philosophical Review* 80, no. 1: 3–27.

———. 1987. *Reasons and Persons*. Oxford: Clarendon Press.

Pope, Devin C., and Maurice E. Schweitzer. 2011. "Is Tiger Woods Loss Averse? Persistent Bias in the Face of Experience, Competition, and High Stakes." *American Economic Review* 101 (February): 129–57.

Senior, Nassau William. 1836. *An Outline of the Science of Political Economy*. London: Clowes and Sons.

Yee, Nick, and Jeremy Bailenson. 2007. "The Proteus Effect: The Effect of Transformed Self-representation on Behavior." *Human Communication Research* 33: 271–90.

Zweig, Jason. 2011. "Meet 'Future You.' Like What You See?" *Wall Street Journal*, March 26.

SAVE MORE

90—**10**—90 GOALS

Average deferral rates into 401(k) plans are about 6 to 7 percent, with young and lower-income workers saving least and older and higher-income workers saving most (Deloitte, 2010; Financial Engines, 2010; PSCA, 2011; Vanguard, 2010). For most people, this is not enough. For instance, according to data compiled by the Federal Reserve and analyzed by the Center for Retirement Research for the *Wall Street Journal*, fewer than one-quarter of households headed by a person aged sixty to sixty two have sufficient funds in their retirement savings accounts to maintain their lifestyles after they retire (Browning, 2011). On the industry side, Financial Engines estimates that almost three-quarters of 401(k) plan participants aren't saving sufficiently to ensure a comfortable retirement (Financial Engines, 2010).

The three chapters in this section describe behavioral interventions designed to overcome the behavioral challenges of inertia, self-control, loss aversion, and myopia that together are largely responsible for low savings rates.

The question we pose here is this: how much should plan participants be saving?

We arrived at a recommended savings rate in three ways. First, we looked at the academic literature. Second, we consulted the opinion of 401(k) experts. Third, we turned to what plan participants themselves say they consider an "ideal" savings rate. The figure we arrived at was a *minimum* of 10 percent. In this section's introduction we will qualify this figure in several ways.

ACADEMIC RESEARCH

We focus on a paper by Roger Ibbotson and his colleagues (2007) titled "National Savings Rate for Individuals." They arrived at recommended savings rates in three calculation steps:

- The annual cash flow needed in retirement.
- The capital needed to generate this lifetime cash flow.
- The saving rate needed to build the required capital.

The researchers assumed an income replacement rate of 80 percent, based on the *2004 Replacement Ratio Study* (AON Consulting, 2004), a figure that is commonly used in the industry. They assumed an inflation rate of 2.5 percent. And they assumed that future Social Security payments would be the same as they are today.

The researchers calculated required savings rates for plan participants between twenty-five and sixty-five years of age, with incomes of $20,000 and higher, assuming retirement at sixty-five. The model was based on a 90 percent probability of success in accumulating the required capital. You can see the results in the accompanying table, adapted from Ibbotson et al., 2007.

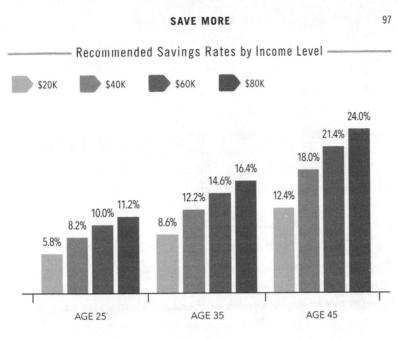

Figure ii–1.

If there is one message that comes through most clearly, it is the need to start saving early. The authors point out that, typically, the recommended savings rate for a person starting to save at age twenty-five more than doubles if they wait until age forty-five and triples for those who don't get around to saving until they reach fifty-five. Those who start saving early face a recommended savings rate that is manageable for most people: barely 6 percent for someone earning $20,000, and just over 11 percent for someone earning $80,000. Ibbotson and his colleagues identify what they call a "critical inflection point" between ages thirty-five and forty. After forty-five, late savers face a challenging uphill struggle, with catching up a distant and rapidly retreating prospect.

Against this background, let us consider the "average" plan participant, whose demographics are as follows:

Average age: 43.8
Median income: $61,940
Mean account balance: $76,020
Median account balance: $24,680*

Using the table from Ibbotson et al., 2007, we find that the average participant with the average account balance should be saving at a rate of about 16 percent.

The average account balance is, however, probably skewed somewhat by a few large accounts, and the many participants who have relatively small balances remain invisible with this measure. The median account balance gives a more meaningful view of most participants' prospects, because it represents the typical participant. In this case the recommended saving rate calculation rises to 19 percent. There will, of course, be a lot of variation among individuals, especially over their age at enrollment.

401(K) EXPERTS

First, let's consider the advice of financial advisers. We asked the 134 401(k) experts in the two surveys we mentioned in the introductory chapter the following question: what percentage of salary do you think a typical 401(k) participant should be deferring in order to reach his or her retirement goals? (See Appendix 1 for survey questions.) We found an average recommendation of 12.3 percent and a median of 12 percent.

Recommendations of savings rates from financial-services providers also vary somewhat. The following figures are to be found on online retirement savings Web sites for workers who begin saving relatively early: a 10 to 15 percent savings rate, described as "a very good start" (Vanguard, 2011); 12 to 15 per-

---

* These figures were provided by Yan Xu and Holli Thoren, AON Hewitt, 2011.

cent of pay, including employer contribution (Fidelity, 2011); and 15 to 25 percent for someone starting saving in their thirties (Schwab, 2011).

WHAT EMPLOYEES SAY

We have found just one academic survey of employees' opinions on retirement savings rate. This involved almost 600 employees at a large U.S. food company who took part in a retirement education meeting. Some were already participating in the company's retirement plan while others were not. They all were asked the following question:

> Based on anything you may have heard or read, what percent of your income do you think you should *ideally* be saving for retirement?

The average response was 13.9 percent. The survey also revealed that two-thirds (67.7 percent) judged their actual saving rate to be inadequate relative to their stated ideal, as we've noted in earlier chapters (Choi et al., 2006)

PLANSUCCESS RECOMMENDATION

Recall that in the introduction to Section One we recommended a goal of 90 percent for plan participation rate, with the possibility of some slight variation because of different employee demographics. We cannot be as precise with the savings rate, for many reasons. As we have seen above, recommended rates from different sources and perspectives vary considerably, which is an indication that there is no single "correct" number. There is no single correct number because there is no one-size-fits-all optimum savings rate for all circumstances.

There are uncertainties and variables that can significantly influence a savings rate target. One uncertainty is whether the commonly assumed replacement ratio of 80 percent is correct. There are reasons to believe that it might be too low. For instance, 214 T. Rowe Price customers who had retired within the last two years were asked whether they needed less money after retirement than before, about the same amount, or more than before. Forty-one percent said they needed about the same income as before, suggesting a perception that their spending needs had not gone down at retirement (Benartzi, 2009).

Another uncertainty is the future of Social Security. It seems increasingly likely that, to keep the system sustainable, future payments will be lower than they have been historically. Both of these factors—a higher than 80 percent replacement ratio and lower future Social Security payments—would imply the need to increase savings. A third uncertainty is future returns on investments. If future returns happen to be lower than the historical returns that are built into most savings rate calculations, then this, too, implies the need for an increased savings rate. Longevity also comes into the equation, as Roger Ferguson, CEO of TIAA-CREF, recently pointed out. Since 2000, longevity has crept up from seventy-seven to seventy-nine, which, he said, implies the need for higher savings rates.

The age at which employees begin saving is perhaps the biggest variable in the equation, as we saw from the Ibbotson study. So, when asked, "How much should I be saving?" the correct response is, "It depends." It depends on how those various uncertainties unfold. And it depends critically on your age.

The bottom line here is that most people aren't saving enough and need to save more. The study by Ibbotson et al. showed clearly that starting to save while one is young is not only sensible, but necessary. Those who wait until age thirty-five or older will likely never catch up, and will face an underfunded retirement. It is very clear to us that the most valuable advice that anyone entering the workplace can receive is this: start saving for your retirement *as early as possible*. In the event that you discover that you are accumulating more capital than you strictly need, then reducing the savings rate is an option. We suspect, however, that saving too much is not a serious danger for the vast majority of people. After all, just 1 percent of people in Choi's survey of employees' opinions on savings adequacy said they were saving too much (Choi et al., 2006).

Based on the figures given from the three sources above, we suggest a saving rate of 10 percent as a *bare minimum target*. We would say it is a good start. This target rate assumes a generous employer match. If there is no employer match, then employees will need to save more than the minimum target. Many workers will, for reasons outlined above, need to save more than 10 percent, often substantially more, as we saw with the calculations for the "average" participant. Plan sponsors should work with their advisers on the appropriate saving rate for their specific plan.

REFERENCES

AON Consulting. 2004. *2004 Replacement Ratio Study*.

Benartzi, Shlomo. 2009. "How Much Is Enough?" *401(k)Now* (Fall): 4–6.

Browning, E. S. 2011. "Retiring Boomers Find 401(k) Plans Fall Short." *Wall Street Journal*, February 19.

Choi, James J., David Laibson, Brigitte C. Madrian, and Andrew Metrick et al. 2006. "Defined Contribution Pensions: Plan Rules, Participant Choices, and the Path of Least Resistance." In *Tax Policy and the Economy*, vol. 16, edited by James Poterba. Cambridge: MIT Press.

Deloitte. 2010. *Annual 401(k) Survey: Retirement Readiness*.

Fidelity.com. 2011. "Am I Saving Enough?" https://401k.fidelity.com/public/content/401k/Home/AmIsavingenough.

Financial Engines. 2010. "National 401(k) Evaluation."

Ibbotson, Roger, James Xiong, Robert P. Kreitler, Charles F. Kreitler, and Peng Chen, et al. 2007. "National Savings Rate Guidelines for Individuals." *Journal of Financial Planning* (April): 50–61.

PSCA. 2011. *54rd Annual Survey*.

Schwab, Charles. 2011. "How Much Should You Save for Retirement? Play the Percentages." http://www.schwab.com/public/schwab/research_strategies/market_insight/retirement_strategies/planning/how_much_should_you_save_for_retirement_play_the_percentages.html.

Vanguard. 2010. "How America Saves."

Vanguard.com. 2011. "Why We Need to Save More." https://retirementplans.vanguard.com/VGApp/pe/PubVgiNews?ArticleName=NeedtoSaveMore.

CHAPTER 4

SAVE MORE TOMORROW™ 1.0

PREVIEW

Three-quarters of 401(k) plan participants are saving too little to ensure a comfortable retirement (Financial Engines, 2010). At the same time, almost as many workers acknowledge they are not saving enough and would like to save more (Choi et al., 2006). Save More Tomorrow™ (SMarT) is a behavioral program whose choice architecture makes it easy for workers to achieve what they say they want—adequate savings for their retirement.

Several behavioral factors lead to workers' suboptimal saving behavior. The first is "present bias," which is the tendency to sharply reduce the importance of the future in decision making. In this case, people greatly prefer to spend now rather than save for the future. This bias also seduces people into believing that doing the right thing in the future would be easier than it is now, because the pain of doing it is discounted in the future. As a result, people end up procrastinating—putting off painful tasks.

Procrastination is linked to inertia, the second behavioral factor at work here. Inertia traps people into continuing to do what they are currently doing, rather than changing their behavior. So, those who are automatically enrolled with a low default savings rate of, say, 3 percent, fail to take action to increase it.

The third behavioral factor involved in low savings rates is loss aversion. People do not like to see their paychecks shrink, which makes them reluctant to increase their contributions to their retirement accounts. We will address loss aversion and increasing retirement savings in Chapter 5.

Richard Thaler and I developed the SMarT program to solve the problem of inadequate saving. The program transforms the above behavioral challenges into behavioral opportunities that help plan participants increase their rate of saving. The first step, which plays into present bias, is to invite participants to join a program that commits them to increase their saving, beginning *at some time in the future*, say, next January. People show themselves to be very willing to do this, because it makes a painful future action easier today.

Once plan participants have committed to saving more in the future, the second step is to adopt automatic annual increases in saving. Inertia, which typically causes problems, is now an ally, keeping people on a trajectory to adequate savings rather than preventing them from getting there.

SMarT works: in the first case study, which began in 1998, savings rates increased from 3.5 percent to 13.6 percent of income over three and a half years. In 2009, 59 percent of large companies in the United States included some form of savings escalator program, up from 1 percent in 2003 (Hewitt, 2010).

BEHAVIORAL CHALLENGES TO SAVING

Standard economic analysis assumes that people are able to calculate how much they will need for a comfortable retirement, and then save sufficiently to meet that goal. That initial assumption, so easily stated, is in fact quite complicated. Some of the factors that must be incorporated into the equation include the following:

- How long the individual will work.
- How long their spouse (if married) will work.
- How long the individual will live.
- How long the spouse will live.
- Lifetime earnings.
- Social Security benefits.
- Future expenses.
- Whether Medicare will adequately cover future medical expenses.
- Expected return on investments.
- Future inflation.
- How much to leave the kids and grandkids.

The theory also assumes that people think carefully about retirement plans and make thoughtful decisions, regardless of the choice architecture involved. It assumes, therefore, that if people are saving very little for their future comfort, this reflects their intent and desires. The introduction and rapid rise to dominance of self-directed retirement plans, such as 401(k) plans, put this model to the test. Reality, it turned out, fell far short of the economists' utopian world.

The reasons are quite simple and, from a behavioral finance view of the world, to be expected. First, without good computer software, even a trained economist would find those calculations daunting, if not impossible. And second, many people lack the self-control required to sacrifice current pleasure for future security (Thaler and Shefrin,1981). Recall that few of us have the self-control of a nun; we find it hard to do the right thing, especially if it requires a sacrifice, no matter how small, in the present. Limited self-control makes it hard for many people to do the right thing and increase how much they are saving. As a result, three-quarters of 401(k) plan participants are not saving enough for their retirement (Financial Engines, 2010). At the same time, two-thirds of employees recognize their savings shortfall and would like to save more (Choi et al., 2006).

Rather than characterize this collective savings shortfall as intentional, as conventional economics might, behavioral finance describes it as a "mistake." It is a mistake in the same way that an individual makes the mistake of not controlling his or her eating, is overweight, and would welcome help in shedding those unwanted pounds. Richard Thaler and I developed the Save More Tomorrow™ (SMarT) program more than a decade ago specifically to address this behavioral mistake around saving more. (As I said in the Introduction, its great success is one reason I chose the same phrase for the title of this book.) SMarT is a behavioral finance program whose choice architecture is designed to help workers overcome their savings mistakes and to make it easy for them to save, without limiting their available choices. Standard economic analysis predicts that workers should have no interest in joining such a program because they are assumed to be saving exactly what they intend to save. Behavioral finance, on the other hand, predicts that many workers would welcome help in boosting their savings; and this is exactly what we see.

Thaler and I identified three key behavioral challenges that cause workers to save insufficiently for retirement (Thaler and

Benartzi, 2004). They are hyperbolic discounting (present bias), inertia, and loss aversion. We will address the first two in this chapter, while loss aversion is the central topic of the following chapter.

Humans have a strong tendency to focus disproportionately on the present and near-term future. The value we place on an object or activity falls off very rapidly as we look into the future, and then it tails off more slowly thereafter, hence the academic term *hyperbolic* discounting (Ainslie, 1992). Hyperbolic discounting could be characterized by the lack of self-control needed to follow one's long-term goals. It also explains why many of us engage in behaviors such as excessive eating, lack of exercise, and excessive spending that feel good in the present but can have unfortunate consequences in the future.

Here's a simple experiment that illustrates the power of temptation in the present. Subjects were told they would be asked to choose between a healthy snack (bananas) and an unhealthy snack (chocolate). When faced with that choice a week in advance, only a quarter said they would be tempted to choose chocolate over bananas. However, one week later, when subjects faced the choice *on the spot*, nearly three-quarters succumbed to temptation, and chose chocolate (Read and Leeuwen, 1998).

"Eat, drink, and be merry, for tomorrow we die" might be a reasonable philosophy for a warrior going into battle, but it is not good advice for the rest of us. Nevertheless, it does aptly describe the power of present bias in many people, as Edward Miller, dean of the medical school at Johns Hopkins University and CEO of Johns Hopkins Medicine, observes. "If you look at people after coronary-artery bypass grafting two years later," Miller told a writer for *Fast Company*, "ninety percent of them have not changed their lifestyle. . . . Even though they know they have a very bad disease and they know they should change their lifestyle, for whatever reason, they can't" (Deutschman, 2005).

Even though saving inadequately for one's retirement is not life threatening (as is the coronary-artery disease example) it is lifestyle threatening. But retirement is way in the future, temporally and psychologically, for most workers, and many find it difficult to place appropriate value on it. They find it difficult to imagine that what they will be doing in their retirement years will measure up to the pleasure they are enjoying in the present. Present bias therefore leads people to procrastinate, saying, "I will start that diet plan *tomorrow*" or "I plan to join the gym *tomorrow*" or "I will definitely do the sensible thing and start saving for my retirement *tomorrow*." "Tomorrow" is often "never."

Procrastination, in turn, produces a strong tendency toward inertia, or status-quo bias. For instance, Samuelson and Zeckhauser found that more than half of the participants in TIAA-CREF, a large retirement plan provider for university and university-related employees, reached retirement with the same allocation of contributions as the day they became eligible to join the plan decades earlier (Samuelson and Zeckhauser, 1988). One extreme example of inertia trumping good sense comes from the United Kingdom, where certain defined benefit plans do not require employees to contribute. Even though the plan is free to employees, they are still required to take action and sign up for the plan. Data from twenty-five such plans show that, remarkably, only half of eligible employees did so.[*]

We can be sure, then, that because of inertia, 401(k) plan participants who are saving inadequately today will more than likely continue to save inadequately tomorrow, unless something comes along and makes it easy for them to change their saving behavior.

We saw in Chapter 1 (and above) that inertia is a powerful force keeping eligible employees from enrolling in 401(k) plans

---

[*] We thank David Blake and the UK Department of Work and Pensions for providing these data.

in the first place. We also saw that this behavioral challenge could be overcome by changing the choice architecture around participation in 401(k) plans: the switch from Auto-Grounded to Auto-Takeoff. The result is dramatic: participation for new hires jumps from between 30 and 70 percent at six months of tenure to between 85 and 95 percent. Inertia now works in employees' best interests, because procrastinators and those with present bias are now saving, which is what most say they want to do.

But inertia in this context has a downside, too. When Brigitte Madrian and Dennis Shea published the very first results on Auto-Takeoff in 2001, they showed that 76 percent of new hires stuck with the default savings rate of 3 percent, compared with 12 percent of participants who had opted into the plan and chose this rate themselves. Even after a year, very few new hires changed their contribution; they continued to stick with the low rate. The authors pointed out the danger that inertia seemed to produce what they called "passive savers" (Madrian and Shea, 2001). By 2011, Auto-Takeoff had become relatively common, and Madrian and Shea's observations had come home to roost.

The Pension Protection Act of 2006 (PPA) contains provisions that encourage employers to adopt Auto-Takeoff, which contributed to its rising popularity. An article in the July 7, 2011, issue of the *Wall Street Journal* reported that 40 percent of new hires are now saving less than if they had opted into their plans rather than participating through Auto-Takeoff (Tergesen, 2011). This was no surprise to me, or to anyone who had thought about the power of inertia, but the article treated it as an unexpected consequence of Auto-Takeoff, and led with the erroneous title, "401(k) Law Suppresses Saving for Retirement."

The PPA prescribes a *minimum* initial contribution of 3 percent, and, at the same time, a *minimum* automatic escalation of savings rate of 1 percent per year, with a target of 6 percent, but no more than 10 percent. Plan sponsors are free to increase these numbers, or take other actions to ensure that participants save at adequate levels, if they so choose. Many do not, perhaps for reasons of inertia, anchoring on the minimum numbers, and the herd effect of doing what others around them are doing. Many plan participants also failed to raise these numbers, perhaps for the same reasons.

The PPA is not perfect, but it did not "suppress" saving. Poor implementation of the law is responsible for participants' suboptimal saving behavior. SMarT offers a solution to this problem by transforming the behavioral challenges that suppress saving into behavioral strategies that make it easy for employees to increase it. Its goal is to have plan participants join a savings escalator program and to obtain some of the advantages of Auto-Takeoff while avoiding some of the disadvantages.

BEHAVIORAL SOLUTIONS THAT MAKE SAVING EASY

As powerful as present bias and inertia can be in preventing plan participants from increasing their saving, they can be equally effective at enhancing saving, when the choice architecture is reformulated. The reformulation appears to be simple, but simplicity is where the power lies with SMarT, because there is a lot of psychology behind it.

Think again about the individual who makes the mistake of carrying around more pounds than he would like, and is looking for help to lose them. We could encourage him to commit to a dietary program in which he would eat only specified amounts of certain foods at home, and visit a prescribed restaurant every Monday evening for a low-cal dinner. (The restaurant has a special menu for him, which displays no tempting desserts.) If he stuck unswervingly to this program, our subject would soon begin shedding those unwanted pounds. But who's to stop him from cheating? Who's to stop him from slipping an éclair into his shopping cart, along with the tofu, carrots, and celery? And who would know if he furtively dropped in to a different restaurant on his Monday night out? A great deal of self-control would be required to succeed on this program, and we know that self-control is typically in short supply.

The ideal way to ensure that the weight loss program would work would be to ask our subject to commit to living on a desert island with just one restaurant that had no desserts on the menu and only healthful foods to choose from. That one commitment, "I will live on a desert island with a diet-conscious restaurant," leads our subject automatically to lose the weight he wants to.

In many ways, SMarT is like that ideal, because it asks employees to make just one commitment. Instead of being asked to agree to live on a desert island where everything works in the dieter's (saver's) best interests, 401(k) plan participants are simply asked to join a savings escalator program, SMarT, that commits them to begin to increase their savings rate *at some time in the future*, thus avoiding the present bias. With that one action, everything else follows automatically: employees' savings rates would be automatically raised by a specified amount at the same time every year, up to a preset cap, thus making good use of inertia. After that initial commitment, participants in the savings escalator program, like the dieter on the desert island, are not required to make any further decisions. All the work is done for them by the plan administrator. The SMarT program therefore transforms the power of inertia from being a barrier to saving to being a facilitator, making it easy to save more. Participants are free to opt out of the program at any time, but experience shows that very few do.

The first implementation of SMarT began in 1998, at a midsize manufacturing company. Seventy-eight percent of the employees who were offered the program elected to join after one-on-one financial counseling on the wisdom of increasing retirement saving. The plan consultant elected a saving increment of 3 percentage points and a total of four annual increases. After three and a half years on the program, this group's average savings rate almost quadrupled, from 3.5 to 13.6 percent of income (Thaler and Benartzi, 2004). Since this group had gone through four pay raises, some individuals increased their savings rate by 12 percentage points. A few program participants dropped out, mostly between the third and fourth pay raises. They maintained their saving at the newly elevated rate but did not reach the maximum possible after the four planned pay raises. The average increase in savings rate was therefore 10.1 percent, not 12 percent.

We will present more details about the implementation of the SMarT program at this company in the following chapter, but it is worth noting here that the people who elected to join the program were, on the face of it, those struggling most to save.

When employees were offered the opportunity to meet with the financial consultant, almost 10 percent declined. The average savings rate for this group at that time was 6.6 percent. Of those who accepted the invitation, 28 percent adopted his advice to boost their saving with an immediate one-time increase of 5 percentage points. Their average savings rate was 4.4 percent at that time. This left a pool of employees who did not feel they could follow the consultant's advice and boost their saving by a 5 percentage-point jump. The average savings rate of this group was 3.5 percent, which is the lowest average for all the employees. Had they accepted the consultant's advice to bump up this low rate by a onetime 5 percentage-point hike, they would have elevated their saving to an average of 8.5 percent.

This last group, the lowest-level savers at the company and the least willing to commit to an immediate onetime saving increase, were then offered the SMarT program. Seventy-eight percent of the these "timid" savers accepted and, as noted earlier, within three and a half years many had increased their savings rate by 12 percentage points, with an average total savings rate of 13.6 percent. Compare this with 6.2 percent after three and a half years for those who declined the consultation, and 8.8 percent for those who accepted the consultant's advice. Note also that the eventual savings rate of the timid savers who had joined the SMarT program was much higher than it would have been had they accepted the consultant's advice. (See Figure 4-1.)

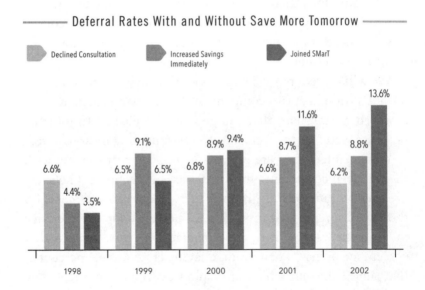

——— Deferral Rates With and Without Save More Tomorrow ———

Declined Consultation   Increased Savings   Joined SMarT
                                 Immediately

Figure 4-1. The saving rate for "timid savers" jumped from an average of 3.5 percent prior to the implementation of the SMarT program to 13.6 percent after three and a half years on the program. (Source: Richard Thaler and Shlomo Benartzi, "Save More Tomorrow: Using Behavioral Economics to Increase Employee Saving," *Journal of Political Economy* 112, no. 1, pt. 2 (2004), pp. S164-S187.)

Skeptics of the outcome of this test case might have been tempted to suggest that the employees who opted for the SMarT program were eager savers at heart, and that we were just tapping into that hidden urge. The above numbers show that assumption to be false. SMarT morphed timid savers into bold savers by transforming behavioral challenges into behavioral solutions.

The power of the SMarT program, given these numbers, is blindingly obvious. This extremely favorable outcome caught the attention of plan sponsors, and SMarT, or similar savings escalator programs, became increasingly popular, rising from 1 percent in large companies in 2003 to 59 percent in 2009 (Hewitt, 2010). Outcomes have varied, however.

The original case just described was in many ways somewhat unusual, which might have favored especially high rates of saving. As already mentioned, it included intensive one-on-one counseling for every employee who wanted it; the SMarT program and its implications were described in great detail; and signing on to the program was made very easy. Most implementations have not been as intense as this first one, and in many cases employees have to jump through procedural hoops, such as multiple clicks through many Web pages, for example, in order to join. Experts in the communications industry recognize that people's attention decays quite significantly as they navigate through Web pages. Every extra click on the way to joining SMarT, for instance, reduces the number of employees who ultimately sign up. When employees face these unintended obstacles, participation rates may sometimes only be in the teens. The key—and the theme of the entire PlanSuccess System presented in this book—is to make it easy for employees to do the right thing. Programs similar to SMarT are being implemented in the United Kingdom, Australia, and New Zealand.

HOW YOU CAN IMPLEMENT
SAVE MORE TOMORROW™ 1.0

Plan sponsors and their advisers face three questions when introducing the SMarT program to their 401(k) plans:

- When is the best time to initiate the first increase in savings rate after plan participants have signed up for the SMarT program?
- How big should the saving increments be?
- What should be the saving cap?

In the first case study described earlier, saving increases were synchronized with pay increases, a formula we will explore in the following chapter. Very often, however, saving and pay increases are not synchronized, for various reasons. In these cases the plan sponsor needs to know what is the optimum time, from the participants' perspective, for the first saving increase to take effect after employees have signed onto the SMarT program.

We know that, because of present bias, most people prefer to put off doing the right thing until some time in the future. And Thaler and I suspected that a strong factor might be at play, specifically in the preference for a particular month of the year during which to start doing "the right thing."

Most readers, after giving a few moments of thought to the matter, would probably come up with the month that we saw favored in a study with data from Vanguard. That's right, January. Of more than 43,000 program participants in the study, 37.3 percent chose January as the preferred month for the first saving increase. Every other month of the year received fewer than 10 percent of votes (Benartzi et al., forthcoming). We suspect that the Western cultural tradition of "turning over a new leaf" with the start of the New Year drives this mental accounting reference point in this context. (See Figure 4-2.) We therefore recommend that no matter when employees sign up for the SMarT program, January should be the date selected for the first saving increase.

How large should saving increments be? In the above case study they were 3 percent, which got program participants to their plan's target very quickly—a desirable outcome. However,

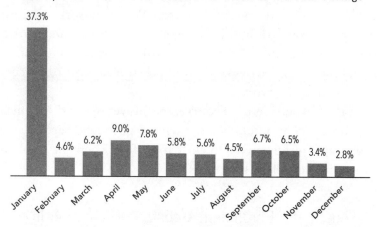

Figure 4-2. Subjects overwhelmingly select January as the month to take action in the future, following a long Western tradition of turning over a new leaf at the beginning of the year. (Source: Benartzi et al., forthcoming.)

loss aversion might be triggered if the saving increase is not syn-chronized with a pay increase; we will address this in the follow-ing chapter. By contrast, the savings escalator provision in the PPA recommends at least 1 percent, a figure that in 2009 three-quarters of plan sponsors apparently took as a prescription, up from 31 percent in 2005 (Vanguard, 2010). With this minimum level of increase, and assuming an initial default savings rate of 3 percent, which is the case with almost 60 percent of plans (Vanguard, 2010), savings escalator program participants won't reach the PlanSuccess goal of 10 percent saving until the seventh year. We consider this to be too slow a rise, and would recom-mend an annual increment of 2 percent, which halves the time for reaching the savings goal.

Recall that in Chapter 1 we made an argument for the initial default savings rate being 6 percent, because plan participants found it just as palatable as 3 percent. Under this formulation, and with a 2 percent annual saving increase, savings escalator program participants will reach the target saving rate of 10 percent after just two saving increases. Plan sponsors who, for whatever reason, balk at this formula, can choose a compromise: an initial saving rate of 4 percent, with two-percentage-point annual increases. Participants would then reach the 10 percent target after three years.

A cap of 10 percent is, of course, the answer to the third question above: What should be the saving cap? By comparison, the saving cap is just 6 percent in close to half (47.5 percent) of plans with savings escalator programs (PSCA, 2011).

Automatic Enrollment Boosts Participation in Savings Escalator Programs

It is well known, as we explained in Chapter 1, that changing the choice architecture for enrolling in 401(k) plans—making joining the plan the default option—dramatically increases plan participation rates. Given the demonstrated efficacy of the SMarT program to help workers achieve an adequate level of saving quite rapidly, it is clearly in most workers' interests to be in the program. Until quite recently, most savings escalator programs required plan participants to make an active decision to opt in, which we call Auto-Holding. By now you would readily predict that changing the choice architecture for joining a savings escalator program to make the default option automatic enrollment would boost participation in the program.

Plan sponsors might therefore want to consider adopting automatic enrollment of 401(k) plan participants in savings escalator programs such as SMarT if they would like to see more of their participants benefit from its savings enhancement effect. Automatic enrollment into a savings escalator program is what we call Auto-Climb. Employees would, of course, be able to opt out of the program if they wished to. As with employees' decisions around Auto-Takeoff, employers should not take an employee's decision to opt out of the SMarT program as final. Employers should ask these opt-outers, "When would you like to start to save more? Next January? A year from now?"

Automatic enrollment of plan participants into a savings escalator program could occur whether participants were automatically enrolled in the 401(k) plan (Auto-Takeoff) in the first place, or whether they were required to opt in (Auto-Grounded). Obviously, a plan that incorporates both Auto-Takeoff *and* Auto-Climb would be optimal in making saving and saving increase decisions as easy as possible for employees. In 2010, 37.9 percent of Auto-Takeoff plans also had Auto-Climb (PSCA, 2011).

The first implementation of automatic enrollment into a SMarT program (Auto-Climb) was in 2003 with the Safelite Group (Thaler and Benartzi, 2004). There was no synchronization between saving and pay increases, and the annual increment was 1 percent. Of 3,640 employees, only 6 percent opted out, 1 percent elected to save more than the default, and 93 percent remained in the program. Since that time, many more such implementations have been carried out, and data from thirteen plans from Vanguard show the strong boost to participation in the savings escalator program delivered by automatic enrollment into savings escalator programs, or Auto-Climb. In the twelve months prior to the implementation of Auto-Climb programs, 25.1 percent of plan participants opted in, compared with 83.5 percent who are in the program in the twelve months following the implementation of Auto-Climb (Benartzi et al., forthcoming). (See Figure 4-3.) These dramatic figures demonstrate once again the power of inertia and the important role of choice architecture in retirement saving programs.

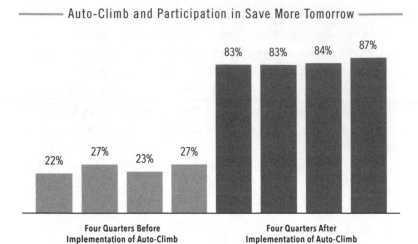

——————— Auto-Climb and Participation in Save More Tomorrow ———————

Figure 4-3. Prior to the implementation of automatic enrollment in the SMarT program (Auto-Climb) around 25 percent of plan participants were on a savings escalator program. With the implementation of Auto-Climb that figure more than tripled. (Source: Benartzi et al., forthcoming.)

COUNTERARGUMENTS

My record keeper does not offer a savings escalator option.

Many record keepers do offer it, as they should, because it is part of the Pension Protection Act of 2006. We recommend that the ability to implement a savings escalator program, preferably Auto-Climb, and other behavioral finance tools, should be an important criterion in selecting a record keeper in the future.

Although my record keeper offers Auto-Climb, it does so only for those employees who have been automatically enrolled in the retirement plan.

That is unfortunate. In such a case, the plan sponsor should consider inviting those employees who are already in the plan by active choice to join the SMarT program. The plan sponsor should ensure that joining SMarT in this way is easy, by following the kind of guidelines used for Easy Enroll, described in Chapter 1. This involves presenting the employee with a simple form with a "yes/no" decision box at the point at which the invitation to join is offered.

Although my record keeper is able to implement a savings escalator program, it declines to handle the required annual notification to program participants of an impending savings rate increase.

We recognize that some record keepers are reluctant to send out these notices, especially when a plan is small and the average account balance is modest. In your negotiations with a potential record keeper, point out that because the goal of the savings escalator program is to boost participants' savings rates to 10 percent, the value of the accounts will rise significantly in just a few years. Encourage the record keeper to plug these numbers into her own revenue model so that she will clearly see that the plan will soon be profitable for her. Once again, the record keeper's willingness to handle the annual notification should be an important criterion in hiring one in the future.

Savings escalator programs, including Auto-Climb, should not only make it easy for plan participants to rapidly increase their rate of saving, it should also be easy for plan sponsors, who should not be involved in headache-inducing administrative chores. This is the job of the record keepers, and many would be delighted to assist.

I am concerned that a saving increment of 2 percentage points is too aggressive and will discourage plan participants from joining the Auto-Climb program.

There is no reason for concern. Research has shown that potential program participants have identical responses to 1 percent and 2 percent increments (Benartzi, 2006). Using a two-percentage-point increment will get program participants to their target savings rate faster.

I am still worried that in difficult economic times, when employees' health and welfare costs are creeping up (reducing their take-home pay), 2 percent is too much to ask of them.

In that case, you have a couple of options. One would be to commit now to join the savings escalator program, with the initial saving increase taking place not this coming January, but the following January. Another would be to commit now to joining the program, with the initial saving increase beginning next January, but at a rate of 1 percent. You could then raise the savings increase to 2 percent the following year.

If I implement SMarT and it succeeds in getting employees who were not saving to the maximum of the employer match to now do so, my plan costs will go up.

That is true, but you can mitigate the increase in your plan costs by adopting the Match Optimizer, described in Chapter 2.

BEHAVIORAL FINANCE ACTIONS

►**Action 1:** Invite plan participants to join the SMarT program, with the first increase to take place the following January 1. For optimum participation in the SMarT program, incorporate automatic enrollment, or Auto-Climb, into the program.

►**Action 2:** Set the annual increment at 2 percent.

►**Action 3:** Set a savings target of 10 percent of pay. We have suggested that the initial savings rate should be 6 percent, which gets participants to the PlanSuccess goal of 10 percent in two years. But if 6 percent is considered too high, plan sponsors could elect to start at 4 percent. Participants then take a year longer to reach the target.

REFERENCES

Ainslie, George W. 1992. *Picoeconomics*. Cambridge: Cambridge University Press.

Benartzi, Shlomo. 2006. "Using Automatic Saving Increases Effectively." *401(K)Now* (Fall).

Benartzi, Shlomo, Ehud Peleg, and Richard H. Thaler. Forthcoming. "Choice Architecture and Retirement Saving Plans." In *The Behavioral Foundation Of Policy*, edited By Eldar Shafir. New Jersey: Princeton University Press.

Choi, James J., David Laibson, Brigitte C. Madrian, and Andrew Metrick. 2006. "Defined Contribution Pensions: Plan Rules, Participant Decisions, and the Path of Least Resistance." In *Tax Policy and the Economy*, vol. 16, edited by James Poterba. Cambridge: MIT Press.

Deutschman, Alan. 2005. "Change or Die." *Fast Company* (May): 1.

Financial Engines. 2010. "National 401(k) evaluation."

Aon Hewitt. 2010. "Hot Topics in Retirement, 2010."

Madrian, Brigitte C., and Dennis Shea. 2001. "The Power of Suggestion: Inertia in 401(k) Participation and Saving Behavior." *Quarterly Journal Of Economics* 116: 1149–1525.

PSCA. 2011. *54rd Annual Survey*.

Read, Daniel, and Barbara Van Leeuwen. 1998. "Predicting Hunger: The Effects of Appetite and Delay of Choice." *Organizational Behavior and Human Decision Processes* 76, no. 2: 189–205.

Samuelson, William, and Richard J. Zeckhauser. 1988. "Status Quo Bias in Decision Making." *Journal of Risk and Uncertainty* 1 (March): 7–59.

Tergesen, Anne. 2011. "401(k) Law Suppresses Saving for Retirement." *Wall Street Journal*, July 7.

Thaler, Richard H., and Shlomo Benartzi. 2004. "Save More Tomorrow™: Using Behavioral Economics to Increase Employee Saving." *Journal of Political Economy* 117: S164–S187.

Thaler, Richard H., and Hersh M. Shefrin. 1981. "An Economic Theory of Self-Control." *Journal of Political Economy* 89: 392–406.

Vanguard. 2010. "How America Saves."

CHAPTER 5

SAVE MORE TOMORROW™ 2.0

PREVIEW

Loss aversion is a bedrock principle of behavioral economics. In the current context, it could be triggered when an annual saving increase to a 401(k) plan decreases take-home pay. The prospect of such a loss might cause employees to be reluctant to join a savings escalator program such as Save More Tomorrow™ (SMarT). An effective solution to this challenge is to synchronize saving increases with pay increases, so that program participants never see the face value of their paychecks shrink. The program participant might say, "Save more when I make more? Yes, I can do that!"

A psychologically attractive formula for synchronization would be to split the pay raise 50/50 between saving and paycheck, with up to 2 percentage points going into savings. Program participants therefore see their paychecks increase once a year (assuming they get an annual pay raise).

Under a savings escalator program in which the entire pay increase goes to savings, however, program participants will see their paychecks remain the same from year to year. They therefore do not experience loss aversion because their paychecks remain unchanged. However, the real value of the paycheck (its buying power) has shrunk by the degree of inflation in the intervening twelve months. If people were to take inflation into account in calculating the value of their paychecks, they would experience loss aversion, because the paycheck's real value is less than it was a year earlier. However, people whose professional lives do not involve paying attention to inflation (most of us) focus only on the nominal value of their dollars, not their real value. Loss aversion is therefore, in reality, nominal loss aversion.

The SMarT program turns this behavioral challenge into a behavioral opportunity for program participants who want to increase their savings rate. Program participants are happy to divert their pay raises to a savings increase as long as there is no decrease in their paychecks' nominal value, even though its real value has diminished slightly. Loss aversion is not triggered.

If synchronization of pay increases with saving increases is not possible for administrative or other reasons, the plan sponsor can fall back on non-synchronization. Synchronization is an attractive feature to have in a savings escalator program, but it is not critical.

SYNCHRONIZATION, OR "SAVE MORE WHEN I MAKE MORE"

Loss aversion, as has been stated more than once, is a bedrock principle in behavioral finance. It refers to the widely demonstrated fact that people typically experience the pain of loss about twice as intensely as they feel the joy of a gain of the same magnitude. This chapter addresses the potential loss aversion that retirement plan participants might experience when they see their paychecks shrink slightly when a small percentage is deferred to savings. This occurs when savings increases take place independently of pay increases. We offer a solution to this behavioral challenge by synchronizing saving increases with pay increases. Under synchronization, or "save more when I make more," employees never see their paychecks shrink in nominal dollars, although there might be some decline in real dollars.

As stated in the previous chapter, the very first implementation of the SMarT program included synchronization of saving increases and pay raises. Here we will look a little more closely at the economic conditions of the employees at that company as a way of introducing the benefits of synchronization.

When Richard Thaler and I were developing the theoretical foundation of the SMarT program in the mid-1990s, we were in conversation with Brian Tarbox, a financial consultant. It took a while to put theory to the test in the real world, and it was Tarbox who eventually found the company that was willing to serve as the test case for our theory.

When Tarbox began discussing the possibility of beginning a trial of SMarT with the company, the average savings rate of its employees in its 401(k) plan was quite low. Management was concerned about this for two reasons. First, because there was no defined benefit plan, workers who were not saving adequately were likely to face bleak retirement prospects. Second, the very low savings rate of the lower-paid, hourly employees constrained how much higher-paid, salaried employees could save, under non-discrimination rules.

In an effort to increase the savings rate of the employees, the company engaged Tarbox to offer one-on-one financial consultation with every employee who was eligible to participate in the retirement savings plan. All but twenty-nine of the company's 315 eligible employees agreed to meet with him. Tarbox used commercial software to compute a desired saving rate for each individual, based on information the employee provided. Tarbox learned from his sessions with employees that "the majority of workers live paycheck to paycheck and can barely make ends meet," so seeing their checks shrink would not be a welcome prospect. Research shows that most people become accustomed to their current level of consumption and expenditure, and this becomes a mental accounting reference point to which we are very sensitive. People balk at the prospect of falling below that reference point, which contributes to loss aversion.

Before he "pressed the button" to compute a savings rate, Tarbox asked each employee if they were willing to increase their deferral rate by more than 5 percent, an arbitrary but reasonable figure he had selected beforehand. For those who were willing to go down that path, Tarbox went on to compute a savings rate, which was often the maximum allowed by the Internal Revenue Service and plan rules. Those who balked at this solution were advised to make an immediate one-time savings increase of 5 percentage points. About a quarter of the employees who met with Tarbox followed one or the other of these recommendations. Those who felt they could do neither were offered the synchronized SMarT program. Slightly more than three-quarters of these timid savers joined the program, with the dramatically improved outcomes on their eventual rate of saving we saw in Chapter 4. This is a significant improvement by any measure.

Tarbox had formulated a quite aggressive saving program for this first test case of SMarT. Participants were to increase their savings rate by 3 percentage points, starting at the next pay increase, which was three months from when the advice was offered and they had signed up. He also ensured that joining the SMarT program was very easy and immediate. We planned to have program participants go through four annual saving increases, coinciding each time with their pay raises. This would get program participants to a robust savings rate very quickly. Typical pay raises at the time were 3.25 percent for hourly employees and 3.5 percent for salaried employees. Those people on the program would therefore see just a small increase in their paychecks, 0.25 to 0.5 percent. But, importantly, they would not see them go down. Loss aversion would therefore be avoided.

As we saw in the previous chapter, the SMarT program transformed timid savers into a group of bold and successful savers. Their savings rates far exceeded those coworkers who had been more willing to save initially, an average of 13.6 percent versus 8.8 percent. The outcome strongly validated the theoretical prediction that Thaler and I had developed. By converting the present bias into a behavioral opportunity, the program succeeded in getting employees to sign up for future saving increases; inertia helped participants stay in the program by automating the future increases, therefore achieving the target savings rate. And synchronizing saving increases with pay raises avoided triggering loss aversion, because paychecks did not go down.

The saving increases in this first test case were, as we've seen, quite aggressive, 3 percent. We would recommend that plan sponsors adopt a different, more modest formula, one that is psychologically very attractive. Namely, pay raises should be

split 50/50 between saving increase and paycheck, up to 2 percentage points into savings. For instance, a pay raise of 5 percent
would be split into 2 percentage points to saving and 3 percentage points to the paycheck. With a pay raise of 3 percent,
employees would see 1.5-percentage point increases in both saving and paycheck.

SYNCHRONIZATION VERSUS NON-SYNCHRONIZATION

The ideal retirement plan would include automatic enrollment
in the plan (Auto-Takeoff) and automatic enrollment in the savings escalator program (Auto-Climb). It would also include synchronization of saving increases with pay increases, as described
here. We recognize that synchronization is not always possible,
for administrative- and bookkeeping-related reasons. During
our research on SMarT, we were interested in how program participants valued synchronized versus non-synchronized program designs. Ideally, we would like to have done a field
experiment in which half the participants of a retirement plan
were offered a savings escalator program with synchronization,
and the other half, non-synchronization. We would then have
been able to measure directly which design is more attractive to
participants. There are, however, practical obstacles to doing
such an experiment.

Instead, with the help of Warren Cormier of the Boston
Research Group, we initiated a survey of 5,246 retirement plan
participants (Cormier, 2006). We wanted to measure participants' interest in the two different plan designs. Half were asked
to record their interest in joining a savings escalator program
in which the first saving increase would occur next January.
The other half were asked the same question, but were told that
saving increases would be synchronized with pay increases.
Thirty-two percent of participants in the first group said they

would be either very interested or extremely interested in joining such a non-synchronized program. Synchronization was slightly more popular, with 38 percent of participants in the second group saying they were very interested or extremely interested (Benartzi et al., forthcoming).

The difference between the two groups—6 percentage points—is statistically significant, but not dramatic. This tells us that nominal loss aversion is a second-order effect in the program. Plan sponsors who find it difficult to include the synchronization feature can therefore feel comfortable setting the saving increase date as January 1. In this case, however, loss aversion may cause participation rates to be a little lower than they otherwise would be. Synchronization is an attractive design feature to have in a savings escalator program, but it is not critical.

NOMINAL LOSS AVERSION

Astute readers may be raising their eyebrows at the earlier assertion that "synchronizing saving increases with pay raises avoids triggering loss aversion, because paychecks do not go down." While it is true that paychecks do not go down in nominal terms, they are of course lower by the rate of inflation in the intervening year—the real value. However, humans have a strong tendency to focus on the face value of numbers and to give scant attention to what psychologists call the "deep structure" behind them.

Although Yogi Berra apparently had a notion of the value-eroding effect of inflation when he quipped, "A nickel ain't worth a dime anymore," most people have a lot of trouble factoring inflation into money calculations, at least in the short term. Most people focus on the nominal value of dollars rather than the inflation-adjusted, or real, value. This has been called the "money illusion," a very old idea in economics.

One reason for this behavioral challenge, suggest Eldar Shafir, Peter Diamond, and Amos Tversky, authors of a classic paper on the topic, is that we are just not used to the concept of units of measure being anything other than constant (Shafir et al., 1997). An inch typically remains an inch, a mile is reliably always a mile, and a rise in temperature to 100° Centigrade is always required to bring a pot of water to boil (at sea level, anyway). We see dollars in a similar light, as being constant in value. And, say the authors of that paper, the "Money illusion . . . arises in large part because it is considerably easier and more natural to think in nominal terms rather than in real terms." Furthermore, the nominal dollar value in front of our eyes is salient, and unless inflation is rampant or the outcome horizon is distant, the nominal view isn't such a bad estimate of real value.

Here is a classic experiment that reveals people's inability to factor inflation into their judgments. It concerns people's judgment of fairness as it relates to pay cuts and pay increases. One group of test subjects was told to imagine a community in which there was no inflation. They were then asked whether a 7 percent wage cut for workers in this community was "fair." A significant majority, 62 percent, judged it to be unfair. Another group was told that there was 12 percent inflation and was asked to judge the fairness of a 5 percent pay raise. The great majority thought it was fair, and only 22 percent declared it to be unfair. In real terms of course, taking inflation into account, the two conditions are identical: workers under the two conditions suffered a 7 percent decline in pay (Kahneman et al., 1986). And yet most people simply don't see the reality behind the numbers. Having a pay raise *feels* good, even if inflation erodes take-home pay, and having a pay cut simply *feels* bad, no matter what lies behind the numbers.

The money illusion, or its equivalent, is ubiquitous, not just for individuals but also in institutions, including the media. The

———————————— Annual Average Gold Prices ————————————

——— Annual Average Gold Price in 2011 Dollars　　　——— Annual Average Nominal Gold Price

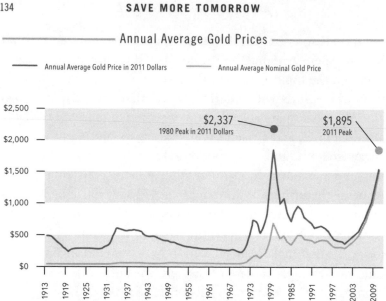

Figure 5-1. The rise of the price of gold in nominal dollars in recent times blinded many people to the fact that, despite the headlines, the peak price of the metal in inflation-adjusted dollars was in 1980, at $2,337 an ounce. (Source: © www.InflationData.com.)

summer of 2011 saw the price of gold rising to what was widely described in business media headlines as an "all-time high." At $1,850 an ounce, it was indeed an all-time high in nominal dollars, but the all-time high in real dollars was reached in 1980. Fueled in part by sky-high inflation following the 1973 oil crisis and a weak U.S. economy, gold soared to $850 an ounce early that year, which, adjusted for inflation, was $2,337 in 2011 dollars. (See Figure 5-1.)

For the same reason, investors pay attention to in-your-face fees such as front-end loads and commissions when buying mutual funds. But they tend to ignore operating costs that are not immediately obvious but whose financial drain can be significant (Barber et al., 2003). The authors of this study aptly titled their paper "Out of Sight, Out of Mind." This is an old idea in psychology, and it has been called the "concreteness principle" (Slovic, 1972). We have a laser-like focus on the numbers in front of our eyes but ignore relevant factors that fall into our peripheral vision.

The bottom line here is that the recognition that the money illusion clouds people's judgment means that when we say loss aversion, we are really talking about nominal loss aversion. People tend to judge gains and losses in nominal rather than real dollars. Participants in a savings escalator program with saving increases synchronized to pay raises therefore accept the fact that their pay packet this year is the same or slightly more in nominal dollars as it was a year ago, even though in real dollars it is somewhat less, in both cases. Loss aversion doesn't kick in because the loss in real terms, to most people, is invisible. The SMarT program turns this behavioral challenge into a behavioral opportunity—helping people do what many say they want to do, which is to save more for their retirement.

COUNTERARGUMENTS

I can see that synchronizing saving increases with pay raises helps avoid loss aversion, but for administrative reasons that would be very difficult, if not impossible, in my case.

Synchronization can be difficult for several reasons. For example, when pay raises occur at different times for different groups of employees, synchronization would be an administrative nightmare. Notification of pay raises is typically a last-minute affair, so record keepers would find it a challenge to coordinate with saving increases. In these cases, and for any other situation where synchronization is a problem, plan sponsors can fall back on non-synchronized saving increases and pay raises, allocating the saving increase to January 1 each year. Synchronization is an attractive feature to have with a savings escalator program, but it is not critical. Many of the benefits of the program are achievable without synchronization.

Some employees might feel upset at seeing some or all of their pay increases being "taken away" by their employer, even though it is going into their retirement savings accounts.

Our formula of a 50/50 split of pay raises into saving (up to 2 percentage points) and paycheck (the balance) ensures that employees always see their paychecks increase when a pay raise is implemented. This should mitigate potential upset on the part of the employees.

This company doesn't have merit increases every year, which means that synchronization wouldn't be possible in "off" years.

In this case you could consider suspending the increase for that year, effectively taking a SMarT holiday, and resuming saving increases with the next pay increase.

BEHAVIORAL FINANCE ACTIONS

▶ **Action 1:** Work with your record keeper to synchronize saving increases with pay raises.

▶ **Action 2:** Split the pay raise 50/50 between savings and pay raise, with up to 2 percentage points going into savings.

▶ **Action 3:** If synchronization proves impossible to implement, fall back on non-synchronization, and make sure that the saving increase takes place on January 1.

REFERENCES

Barber, Brad M., Terrence Odean, and Lu Zheng. 2003. "Out of Sight, Out of Mind: The Effect of Expenses on Mutual Fund Flows." *Journal of Business* 78, no. 6: 2095–2119.

Benartzi, Shlomo, Ehud Peleg, and Richard H. Thaler. Forthcoming. "Choice Architecture and Retirement Saving Plans." In *The Behavioral Foundation of Policy*, edited by Eldar Shafir. New Jersey: Princeton University Press.

Cormier, Warren. 2006. "BRG 2006 401(k) Participant Satisfaction Study." Boston: Boston Research Group.

Kahneman, Daniel, Jack L. Knetsch, and Richard H. Thaler. 1986. "Fairness as a Constraint on Profit Seeking." *American Economic Review* 76: 728–41.

Shafir, Eldar, Peter Diamond, and Amos Tversky. 1997. "Money Illusion." *Quarterly Journal of Economics* 112, no. 2: 341–74.

Slovic, Paul. 1972. "From Shakespeare to Simon: Speculation—and Some Evidence—about Man's Ability to Process Information." *Oregon Research Institute Bulletin* 12, no. 3: 1–29.

CHAPTER 6

THE IMAGINE EXERCISE

PREVIEW

Chapter 3 described how a Behavioral Time Machine solution, the Face Tool, helps people emotionally engage with their future selves, thereby closing the identity gap between the present and future selves. This chapter describes another Behavioral Time Machine tool, the Imagine Exercise, which helps people emotionally engage with their future lifestyle experiences.

For obvious reasons, most people are well aware of their current lifestyle and their experience of it. It feels very tangible. By contrast, because of myopia, or present bias, many people have only a vague appreciation of their future lifestyle in retirement. It feels very intangible and is hard to bring to mind. As a result of this "tangibility gap," increasing saving for retirement now for an adequate accumulation later is often very difficult.

The Imagine Exercise harnesses the power of the imagination with a seemingly simple but effective two-step behavioral process that takes just four minutes. In the first step, employees take two minutes to imagine a financially secure retirement future; in the second step, they spend two minutes writing down what comes to mind in tangible terms, and their emotional response to it. They then record their willingness to increase their saving rate. In a test of the exercise, many subjects said they would increase their current saving by an average of 4.4 percentage points, or more than 70 percent.

The Imagine Exercise helps people transform something intangible—the vague, distant, and, to many people, scary prospect of retirement years—into something tangible, or at least vivid. When something about the future is vivid in our minds, we experience it as being tangible, and we're better able to make good decisions about it in the present.

One of the strengths of the Imagine Exercise is that the images of future lifestyle that people see are, by their nature, customized to each individual's tastes and desires: those images come from their own imaginations. The thrust of this chapter, however, is the need to find ways for people to connect emotionally to their future lifestyle experiences. This helps them make good decisions now about saving more for their retirement. The Imagine Exercise is but one way to do that; we describe others that do the same thing. Plan sponsors may prefer still others. We support whatever choice is made, just as long as connection to future lifestyle experience is achieved.

IMAGINATION, KIDS, AND MARSHMALLOWS

Recall that in Chapter 3 we saw that because of myopia, or present bias, most people find it very hard to identify with their future selves. One's future self can appear to be a stranger to the present self. As a result of this identity gap, joining a retirement savings plan is often a challenge: it can feel like the present self foregoing spending now and "giving" savings to that stranger in the future. We showed how the identity gap could be closed with a Behavioral Time Machine solution, the Face Tool.

In this chapter we address a similar, related behavioral challenge: most people's inability to bring to mind clearly their desired lifestyles in retirement, and to experience those lifestyles emotionally. Trying to compare our emotional experience of today's lifestyle to our experience of that future lifestyle is like comparing apples to oranges. Today's emotional experiences are, by their nature, very tangible to us. In contrast, emotions projected into the future are vague and intangible, and we find it hard to fully grasp them mentally. As a result of this tangibility gap, increasing saving now for a desired future lifestyle is often very difficult. In this chapter we present a behavioral intervention that closes the tangibility gap so that we can now compare apples with apples. The intervention works by harnessing the power of the imagination with a seemingly simple but effective behavioral tool, the Imagine Exercise. As a result, most people are willing to save more now, with the goal of financing a comfortable retirement future.

We introduce the concept of the intervention with a description of a classic experiment in developmental psychology that was developed more than four decades ago. It concerns marshmallows. Or, more specifically, it examines one's ability to delay immediate gratification, using the promise of a greater reward in the future to compensate for successfully delaying gratification. Walter Mischel, now at Columbia University, described the experiments, along with some follow-up observations, with two colleagues in *Science* in 1989 (Mischel et al., 1989).

Who do you think the authors had in mind when they wrote the following description: "impulse-driven . . . unable to delay gratification, oblivious to reason and reality, and ruled entirely by a pleasure principle that demands immediate gratification." Sounds a little like the behaviorally challenged workers we've been describing in earlier chapters, doesn't it, struggling as they are with decisions about saving for retirement? In fact it was a century-old characterization of infants and young children. For the subjects of Mischel's investigation were 653 four-year-old children at the Bing Nursery School on the campus of Stanford University over a period of several years. Self-control is an important behavioral trait. It governs how well we are able to navigate decisions and choices in the world and make plans for the future. As mentioned, self-control is in short supply in infants and young children, but it increases with age, to a greater or lesser degree. People with good self-control tend to do better in many aspects of life—for example, the academic and social spheres—than those with less self-control.

Mischel and his colleagues tested the Bing children's self-control with various tempting objects, such as attractive toys, cookies, and candy. The test that became famous involved marshmallows. One by one, the children sat at a table in a small, bare room, with one marshmallow on a plate in front of them. The experimenter then struck a deal with each child, one at a time. They could eat the marshmallow now, or, if they waited while he left the room for a few minutes and the children left the marshmallow uneaten on the plate during that time, they would get two marshmallows when he returned. The children were told that if temptation got

—— Three Strategies in the Face of Marshmallow Temptation ——

Figure 6-1.

the better of them while he was away, and they felt they could wait no longer, they could ring a little bell and he would return. They could then eat that single marshmallow.

The children's heroic efforts to beat back temptation were caught on camera. Although the experience no doubt was psychologically challenging for the kids, their antics were quite hilarious. Some of them didn't even make any attempt to ring the bell to summon the researcher back in the room and had the tasty morsel in their mouths before the door was barely closed. The more patient ones invented various tricks to delay gratification, such as putting their hands over their eyes or turning the chair around so that the "hot emotion," as psychologists call it, was out of sight, and perhaps out of mind. One girl put her chin on the table and stared intently at the marshmallow, which was just inches from her nose. One boy stroked the little white cushion as if it were a pet. Another picked it up, licked the sugar coating, and put it back on the plate, gnashing his teeth in anguish. Although these videos are not available for public view, a recent rendition of the experiment can be seen on YouTube. Different kids, same antics.

In the original experiment, only 30 percent of the children in the study were able to wait the full fifteen minutes the experimenter stayed out of the room. They were duly rewarded with two marshmallows. As mentioned, some succumbed immediately and ate the marshmallow without waiting. For the rest, the average time before they rang the bell was six minutes. When the marshmallow, the "hot emotion," was either absent or represented by a drawing, however, children were able to wait twice as long as when the temptation was in full view.

For our purposes, the experiment became most interesting and pertinent to developing a behavioral solution to present bias when it involved a simple but powerful twist. The experimenters put a marshmallow in front of the children, as previously, but suggested that they imagine it as something abstract, such as a picture of a marshmallow, or maybe a cloud. Under these circumstances the children were able to wait close to eighteen minutes, compared with just six minutes when they didn't do this little exercise. In their minds, the children had transformed something tangible (the marshmallow) into something intangible (a picture of a marshmallow), an exercise that allowed them to modify their behavior and exert self-control.

When we were developing our own Imagine Exercise in the retirement savings context, one of our team, Sheena Iyengar of Columbia University, brought up the marshmallow experiment and suggested that we take this process, but turn it around: we would harness the power of the imagination to transform something intangible (our experience of retirement lifestyle) into something tangible, or at least vivid (a clear understanding of that lifestyle experience). Again, when something is vivid in our minds we experience it as being tangible.

There is a lot of literature in psychology about the power of vividness to engage people emotionally and affect their behavior (Loewenstein, 1996). For instance, while smoking rates are generally lower among doctors than in the rest of the population, they are especially low among those whose specialty is diseases of the lung. "Daily confrontation with blackened lungs undoubtedly increases the frequency and intensity of negative emotions associated with smoking," wrote George Loewenstein.

An example of the impact of vividness in the financial realm is investors' behavior immediately following a commercial airplane crash. The average U.S. stock market loss after a U.S. airliner crash in which more than seventy-five people are killed is $60 billion. The actual economic loss associated with such disasters is just $1 billion, incurred by the airline, the insurer of the airline company, and the airplane manufacturer. The disparity between the losses caused by the crash itself and the response of investors is the result of anxiety (Kaplanski and Levy, 2010). Fear of flying is widespread, despite its proven safety compared with driving a car. And nothing brings that fear and anxiety to mind more vividly than images and reports of wrecked planes and broken bodies. Vividness has the power to engage emotions and change behavior. In this case it impels investors to be overcautious and pessimistic, and to sell more than they should in the short term. Small and riskier stocks suffer most, along with the stock of the airline company whose plane crashed.

But as Loewenstein noted, vividness can be evoked by stimuli that are not in the external environment. It can be evoked by concentrating intensely on some object or experience set in the future and then engaging the imagination. Such an exercise, he suggested, engages one's emotions in the present, which brings the future into vivid focus so that future emotions may be experienced or predicted.

Research shows that people differ in their ability to make such predictions, or what Gergana Nenkov calls "elaboration on potential outcomes" (Nenkov et al., 2008). People who find it easier to elaborate on potential outcomes are better able to exert self-control over present decisions. Earlier research showed that the act of directing attention to future goals (and their implications) generally improves people's level of self-control (Baumeister et al., 1994). In the present context we are talking about directing attention to, and bringing into vivid focus, our emotional experience of lifestyle in retirement.

IMAGINATION, ADULTS, AND SAVING

Here we present two exercises that close the tangibility gap between present and future lifestyles, and lead people to increase how much they say they intend to save for retirement. The first is one in which I was involved, along with Alessandro Previtero of the University of Western Ontario, and Sheena Iyengar. We call it the Imagine Exercise. The second was developed by Nenkov and her colleagues, Jeffrey Inman and John Hulland, using the Elaboration on Potential Outcomes (EPO) exercise. Both exercises are, essentially, Behavioral Time Machine tools. We will see, first, the power of the imagination to make future experience tangible, thereby improving people's present-day decisions regarding retirement. Second, we will see that the techniques are apparently quite simple and easy to use. But, again, there is a lot of psychology behind them.

The Imagine Exercise

The use of images of lifestyle in retirement is quite common in the financial industry: a couple happily relaxing on the balcony of their condo; a woman energetically grubbing about in her luxuriant flower bed, a nice house in the background; two guys playing a round of golf; a couple hiking in the Rockies; another couple playing with the grandkids; and so on. This is an honest attempt to bring the tangible future experience to mind in the present, with the goal of prompting people to ask if they should be saving more for their retirement. One problem with this approach is that tastes differ: life in a condo is not for everyone, likewise spending hours tending a garden. Some will look forward to vigorous vacations in the great outdoors, but that is not for everyone, either. Ideally, the "vivid images" route to ensuring adequate retirement savings should be customized to each individual's tastes and desires. The Imagine Exercise effectively does that.

Previtero, Iyengar, and I began our research project with a collaboration with *Money* magazine. It was an online survey that featured the following questions:

- What do you fear most about retirement?
- What is the best-case scenario for your retirement?

We distilled the answers and arrived at the top four statements each for the "positive" and "negative" scenarios, which are shown below in Figures 6-2 and 6-3. Pride looms large in the negative scenario, with 49 percent of people fearing the prospect of having to ask their children for financial support. The next category—being unable to pay for an expensive medical procedure—lags far behind, with 24 percent. On the positive side, the majority (60 percent) of people simply want a comfortable life, free from financial worries. Only 25 percent were looking to expand their horizons with travel or hobbies they hadn't had time for in their working lives. It is interesting to note that Previtero found it challenging to have people come up with positive scenarios for retirement, let alone bold, positive scenarios. Out of a sample of several thousand people, fully 40 percent admitted they could see *nothing* positive about retirement: We will be old—what's positive about that?

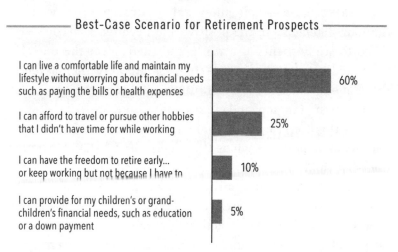

Worst-Case Scenario for Retirement Prospects

I cannot afford living expenses and need to ask my children for financial support — 49%

I cannot afford to pay for a very expensive medical procedure for myself or my spouse — 24%

I cannot afford to help my son or daughter pay for a very expensive medical procedure — 17%

I cannot afford to live in my house and must sell it to live somewhere less expensive — 10%

Figure 6–2.

Best-Case Scenario for Retirement Prospects

I can live a comfortable life and maintain my lifestyle without worrying about financial needs such as paying the bills or health expenses — 60%

I can afford to travel or pursue other hobbies that I didn't have time for while working — 25%

I can have the freedom to retire early... or keep working but not because I have to — 10%

I can provide for my children's or grand-children's financial needs, such as education or a down payment — 5%

Figure 6–3.

The four statements in the positive and negative scenarios were then used in an experiment the three of us carried out in collaboration with the ING Retirement Research Institute. The goal of the experiment was to discover which, if any, of the scenarios—positive or negative—would prompt people more effectively to agree to save more for their retirement. This would help us shape the ultimate Imagine Exercise.

Four hundred employees took part in the experiment, which was part of a series of enrollment meetings for the company's 401(k) plan, divided into five groups. One group saw a single positive statement, which was the first in the list of four above, while the second saw all four positive statements. We used the same formula with the third and fourth groups for the negative statements. The subjects who saw the single statement were asked to spend two minutes thinking about it, and then take another two minutes to write down whatever came to mind *in tangible terms*. They were also asked to write down how they *felt* about the scenario—their emotional response. Subjects who saw the four statements in the positive and negative scenarios were asked to study them for a while and then select the one that resonated most strongly with them. They were then asked to think about that one for two minutes, and to write down what came to mind tangibly and emotionally, as before.

After this exercise, subjects answered some questions around demographic points, such as their age, marital status, whether they had children, and so on. They then had to say whether or not they were currently enrolled in a retirement plan. Those who were not enrolled were asked if they would join now, and if they said yes, they were asked how much they would elect to save. Subjects who were already enrolled in the plan were asked how much they were currently saving, if they now planned to save more, and if they said yes, how much more. A fifth group of subjects, the "control" group, filled in the demographic survey and saving status and intentions but did not see the positive or negative scenarios of the Imagine Exercise.

Here are the outcomes of the exercise. The figures give the percent of people in each group who said they now intend to save more:

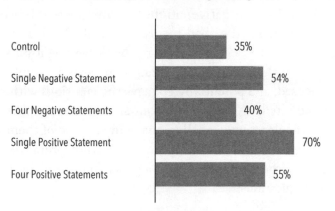

Figure 6–4.

The first thing to notice is that each of the groups that did the Imagine Exercise, regardless of whether they saw positive or negative scenarios, reported a greater intention to save more than the control group, which had only done the demographic survey.

Second, single statements (positive and negative) were more effective motivators than a group of four statements, with the single positive statement being most effective of all. Before the exercise, the average saving for those already in the retirement plan was about 6 percent of pay. The average intended saving *increase* in the group that saw the single positive statement was 4.4 percentage points, which is a jump of more than 70 percent. This is a significant improvement. It highlights the power of the simple, easy-to-implement exercise. The power, of course, lies in engaging each individual's imagination. And we can speculate that the positive statements are more effective than the negative ones because they prompt subjects to realize that perhaps there is something positive about their retirement years.

Why would single statements be more influential than four

statements? After all, one could speculate that having more scenarios (positive or negative) might be more powerful, because there are more good or bad futures to think about. Previtero conjectures that the opposite might be at play. With a single statement to think about, the Imagine process is simpler and more focused, and potentially engages the emotions with some depth and intensity. Faced with four statements, people might find it difficult to emotionally engage in any one of them with equal intensity. Research supports this interpretation. For instance, Norbert Schwarz began a paper some years back with these two questions:

> Who perceives a higher personal risk of heart disease?
> 1) Man A, who is asked to think of three risk-inducing behaviors he engages in? Or 2) man B, who is asked to think of eight such behaviors?

Intuition, and models of judgment and decision making, would opt for Man B. Surely the perception of risk would be higher for the person who thinks of more risky behaviors rather than fewer. When subjects go through this exercise, however, it is those who are asked to think about fewer riskier behaviors that in the end perceive greatest risk, counterintuitive though this may seem. The explanation offered is that bringing to mind three risky behaviors is mentally easier than dredging up eight, and the individual thinks, "Well, I must be at risk." (Schwarz, 2005). The bottom line here is that cognitive ease is powerful in influencing how we think and make decisions. By cognitive ease we mean the ease with which the thought in question comes to mind. It has been called "cognitive fluency."

This, then, is the Imagine Exercise, which we have shown to be quite effective at closing the tangibility gap between present and future experience of lifestyle. As a result, subjects in the experiment said they intended to increase their savings rate by a significant amount. The Imagine Exercise is but one way to achieve this goal. Here is an alternative exercise, developed by Nenkov and her colleagues.

Elaboration on Potential Outcomes Exercise

Remember the marshmallow experiment, which showed that some kids have greater self-control in the face of temptation than others? Walter Mischel and his colleagues found that kids with strong self-control grew up to be adults with good self-control, too. And this, essentially, is what Nenkov and her colleagues are tapping into with Elaboration on Potential Outcomes (EPO). They developed an EPO scale from one to seven, based on people's responses—"strongly disagree" to "strongly agree"—to six questions like these:

- Before I act, I consider what I will gain or lose in the future as a result of my actions.
- I try hard to predict how likely different consequences of my decisions might be.

A person with a score of 7 is a paragon of self-control who always considers the future consequences of present actions and never does anything foolish that will result in regret. Having a score of 1 means you will always be doing the equivalent of popping the marshmallow in your mouth before the door closes, no matter what decision you face. Nenkov and her colleagues did a study of ninety-five volunteers who were invited to take part in a thought experiment. This involved taking the EPO measurement process and then responding to a questionnaire. It asked subjects to imagine they had recently joined a company that offered a 401(k) plan. They were told that they had $15,000 in discretionary income that they could spend as they wished, or they could invest some or all of it in the plan. In one group of volunteers, people with a "high" EPO put an average of $11,006 into the retirement plan, compared with $6,500 for those with a "low" EPO. This is just what one might predict.

A second group underwent "EPO priming," which involved doing the following exercise:

> Please take a moment to think about the potential future outcomes of choosing to invest or not invest in the proposed 401(k) plan. In the space provided below, please list as many outcomes as you can think of, both positive and negative.

Simple though it sounds, it is in fact based on well-established psychology, which goes by the grand-sounding title of Gollwitzer's Deliberative Mind-Set Priming. It effectively engages the imagination to close the tangibility gap between today's world and, in this case, one's future retirement world. As a result of the EPO priming exercise, people with a low EPO score now were willing to save $10,368, which is 60 percent higher than EPO-challenged people in the first group. Interestingly, high-rating EPO people said they would save essentially the same amount as in the non-primed group. They had, apparently, already thought about their future needs, and they took action accordingly. EPO priming therefore seems to help those who most need help.

Although these are hypothetical situations, they do appear to reflect the real world. Gergana Nenkov and her colleagues found that people with a high EPO were "significantly more likely to have a 401(k) type of plan" than EPO-challenged folk. They had, apparently, exercised self-control in real life, and had wisely opted to forego some pleasures today in favor of a financially secure retirement (Nenkov et al., 2008).

So this second exercise designed to close the tangibility gap, like the Imagine Exercise, also works quite effectively. There are probably many others, too. The key for a successful exercise is to find a way to make the future tangible and engage participants' emotions. For instance, here is an example in another context where engaging present emotions about future actions influences behavior. It concerns increasing savings among low-income workers in India. At the end of the work week, workers receive their pay in cash, divided into two envelopes: one is designated for living expenses, the other for savings. Digging into the "savings" envelope causes people to feel guilty, which helps them save when they would otherwise spend. The effect is greatly enhanced, however, when the savings envelope has a picture of the worker's child on it (Soman and Cheema, forthcoming). The emotional strength of the parent/child relationship is powerful.

The point here is not to find a way of using pictures of offspring on envelopes to help employees save more in their retirement accounts. It is that people's emotions about future experiences can be engaged in many simple ways. The Imagine Exercise is just one of those ways, as are the others mentioned. The specifics of the Imagine Exercise are therefore not as important as the concept behind it, namely, using the power of the imagination to make people's experience of future lifestyles tangible in their minds in the present. Plan sponsors and financial advisers could think of other ways to do that, such as coming up with a different narrative that achieves the same ends, as long as it uses imagination in some way.

IMPLEMENTING THE IMAGINE EXERCISE

Based on the above research, this section presents the design of the Imagine Exercise in the workplace.

Give employees a single piece of paper or allow them to do the entire exercise online. The exercise should have the following statements and question at the top:

> Suppose that you decide to save adequately for your retirement. As a consequence, you will be able to live a comfortable life and maintain your lifestyle without worrying about financial needs, such as paying the bills or paying for health-related expenses.
>
> How would you feel about this situation?
>
> Take two minutes to think about your response and a further two minutes to write down in the space below everything that comes to mind, in terms of *tangible* life-style and how you *feel* about it.

In the experiment described earlier, subjects were recording their future saving *intentions*, not their ultimate actions. In order to optimize the efficacy of the Imagine Exercise in real-world situations, it should be undertaken at the point of decision. It is important that employees be encouraged to take action on the spot, immediately after completing the exercise. They do this by checking a "yes" box for the intention to save more on the appropriate paper form or online. They should then indicate the size of the increase by checking one of two boxes in front of them. The first box would indicate 2 percent, which is the size of the savings increase we recommend. There would be a second, empty box. Participants are invited to enter the savings rate increase they prefer if 2 percent is not attractive.

If for any reason a plan sponsor is not happy with these options, they can easily be modified. There could, for instance, be four boxes. The first three would indicate 3, 2, and 1 percent, respectively, while the fourth would be left empty, allowing participants to choose another savings rate.

In summary, the power of the Imagine Exercise is twofold. First, it is the power of the imagination to make vivid and tangible what previously was vague and intangible, namely, the tangible circumstances of one's future retirement life. Second, the images that come to people's minds are, by their nature, "customized" to each individual, because they are the product of each individual's own mind. They are not imposed from the outside by a well-meaning plan provider.

Mischel was quoted recently as saying the following about his marshmallow experiment and its relevance to the world:

> "If you can deal with hot emotions, then you can study for the SAT instead of watching television. And you can save more for retirement. It's not just about marshmallows" (Lehrer, 2009).

COUNTERARGUMENTS

I'm not sure I have the time or resources to administer the process.

If time and resources are limited, plan sponsors might want to outsource the exercise to their record keepers. These days, however, more and more plan sponsors want to be involved in such processes, because they care about their employees' retirement futures. In these cases, the HR director will want to collaborate with the record keeper, and perhaps the financial adviser, in running the event. Whoever administers the exercise, it is always important to ensure that employees are encouraged to take action on the spot, by filling in the appropriate form either on paper or on the record keeper's Web site.

I am not certain about when I am supposed to have my employees do the Imagine Exercise.

The optimum time would be at a 401(k) education or enrollment meeting, when plan participants are being encouraged to think about their retirement plan decisions and take action by enrolling or by increasing their savings rate.

If the Imagine Exercise succeeds in increasing employees' savings rates, my plan costs will increase.

You can control any plan cost increase by implementing the Match Optimizer described in Chapter 2.

I am skeptical that the exercise will work as well in the workplace as it does in a test situation.

That's a valid point, because getting people to act on their intentions is not always easy. We would be very happy to repeat the test where actions would be closely monitored. We invite plan sponsors to volunteer to take part in such a test.

BEHAVIORAL FINANCE ACTIONS

►**Action 1:** At a retirement plan education meeting, or on some other suitable occasion, invite participants to do the Imagine Exercise. The exercise should be outlined either on one piece of paper, or exist as a designated Imagine Exercise page on the plan provider's Web site. Tell them the exercise will take four minutes, and ask them to follow the instructions written either at the top of the paper or on the screen. They are:

Suppose that you decide to save adequately for your retirement. As a consequence, you will be able to live a comfortable life and maintain your lifestyle without worrying about financial needs, such as paying the bills or paying for health-related expenses.

How would you feel about this situation?

Take two minutes to think about your response and a further two minutes to write down in the space below everything that comes to mind, in terms of *tangible* lifestyle and how you *feel* about it.

►**Action 2:** If the plan sponsor prefers a different exercise that's designed to emotionally engage employees in the experience of their retirement lifestyle, such as Nenkov's or another, implement that one.

►**Action 3:** Encourage those who have completed the Imagine Exercise or an alternative exercise to check the "yes" box on a form indicating that they wish to increase their savings rate. Invite those who wish to save more to indicate how much by checking a box on the decision form (hard copy or online). It might be a choice between two boxes, one indicating a two-percentage-point increase in savings rate and the second one left blank, allowing the participant to insert the preferred increase. Or there might be four boxes, three of them offering specified rate increases of 3, 2, and 1 percentage points, and the fourth box blank.

REFERENCES

Baumeister, Roy F., Todd F. Heatherton, and Dianne M. Tice. 1994. *Losing Control: How and Why People Fail at Self-regulation*. San Diego: Academic Press.

Kaplanski, Guy, and Haim Levy. 2010. "Sentiment and Stock Prices: The Case of Aviation Disasters." *Journal of Financial Economics* 95: 174–201.

Lehrer, Jonah. 2009. "Don't." *The New Yorker* (May 18).

Loewenstein, George. 1996. "Out of Control: Visceral Influences on Behavior." *Organizational Behavior and Human Decision Processes* 65, no. 3: 272–92.

Mischel, Walter, Yuichi Shoda, and Monica L Rodriguez. 1989. "Delay of Gratification in Children." *Science* 244: 933–38.

Nenkov, Gergana Y., J. Jeffrey Inman, and John Hulland. 2008. "Considering the Future: The Conceptualization and Measurement of Elaboration on Potential Outcomes." *Journal of Consumer Research* 35: 126–41.

Schwarz, Norbert. 2005. "When Thinking Feels Difficult: Meta-cognitive Experiences in Judgment and Decision Making." *Medical Decision Making* 25, no. 1: 105–12.

Soman, Dilip, and Amar Cheema. Forthcoming. "Earmarking and Partitioning: Increasing Saving by Low-income Households." *Journal of Marketing Research*.

SAVE SMARTER

90—10—**90** GOALS

The challenge of constructing a well-diversified 401(k) portfolio is daunting, even for financial professionals. We believe that a substantial proportion of plan participants have neither the knowledge nor the desire to be their own portfolio manager, and would prefer to delegate the task to an expert. In this introduction to Section Three we ask what proportion of plan participants would be best served by being automatically invested in a one-stop, professionally managed investment vehicle, such as a target date fund or a managed account.

As with the two previous calculations of PlanSuccess goals—for participation and saving rates—here we draw on three lines of evidence. First is academic research into how well participants perform when they act as their own portfolio manager. Second, we sought the opinion of 401(k) experts, the 134 financial advisers we surveyed, as described in the Introduction. Finally, we look at data on how knowledgeable plan participants are about the world of finance and investing, and what they say they would prefer.

ACADEMIC RESEARCH

My colleague Richard Thaler and I conducted a study at Swed-ishAmerican Health System where, upon enrollment in the company's retirement plan, all employees are offered a portfolio selected by ProManage, customized to each individual's demo-graphics (Benartzi and Thaler, 2002). More than a third (36 percent) preferred instead to build their own portfolios. This, then, was a group of participants who not only felt themselves capable of being their own portfolio manager, but also believed they would be able to find the time required to do it.

Our goal was to find out how satisfied these people were with the portfolios they had self-constructed. We asked them to eval-uate three unlabelled portfolios, based on the range of projected income at retirement, on a scale of 1 to 5, with 5 being best. One of the portfolios was their own self-constructed portfolio; the second was the average portfolio of the group; the third was the portfolio that had been customized for each individual by Pro-Manage. The subjects were unaware of the identities of the three unlabeled portfolios.

The results were clear. Although subjects rated their own portfolio and the average portfolio about the same (2.75 versus 3.03 respectively), they showed a strong preference for the one that had been customized for them by ProManage (3.50). Only 20 percent of subjects preferred their own portfolio, whereas 61 percent preferred the customized portfolio, and 19 percent were indifferent. In other words, fully 80 percent of subjects either strongly preferred the professionally constructed portfolio over their own, or were indifferent.

Remember, these people had actively chosen to pass up the option of the customized portfolio, which they now preferred, and opted to construct their own, believing, presumably, that they would do a better job, or at least would be happier. Neither, apparently, was true.

401(K) EXPERTS

We asked the 134 401(k) experts in our two surveys the following question:

> In a typical plan, what percentage of participants would be better off selecting one-stop portfolio solutions, such as target-date funds or model portfolios, instead of self-constructing their own mix of funds?_____%

The average was 83 percent, with a median of 90 percent. Thus, 401(k) experts feel that only one in ten plan participants should construct his own portfolio.

WHAT EMPLOYEES KNOW (OR DON'T KNOW)

A 2002 survey of 801 plan participants by John Hancock Financial Services asked the following question: What type of securities are found in a money market fund? While 45 percent of respondents said that they contain short-term securities, only 8 percent knew that this is all they contain. Some 10 percent believed that money market funds contained stocks, and 47 percent said they included bonds. In other words, fully 92 percent of plan participants did not know what a money market fund is (Hancock, 2002). Given this widespread lack of even the most basic knowledge of the world of investing, it is clear that expecting most participants to construct a well-diversified portfolio is unrealistic.

Indeed, the majority of people do not want to be actively involved in managing their own investments. A recent survey of 1,041 plan participants by JP Morgan suggests that most people prefer not to manage their own portfolio (JP Morgan, 2011): 69 percent say they don't read investment information that is provided for them; 63 percent would welcome a professional to manage the assets in their 401(k) accounts; and 79 percent believe that a target-date fund would be a good solution for them. Clearly, most people don't want to be engaged in investment decisions and would prefer to delegate that responsibility to a professional. Most participants want to be what we are calling "delegators."

PLANSUCCESS RECOMMENDATION

What proportion of participants are best served by being in the delegator class? The three lines of evidence above give numbers that vary between 80 and 90 percent. We will err on the conservative side and opt for 90 percent. For this class of participants, automatic investment in a one-stop, professionally managed, well-diversified investment vehicle is the optimal behavioral solution. Participants are, of course, free to opt out if they so choose. In addition, plan sponsors and their advisers can tailor the 90 percent goal to their specific population of plan participants.

REFERENCES

Benartzi, Shlomo, and Richard H. Thaler. 2002. "How Much Is Investor Autonomy Worth?" *The Journal of Finance* 57, no. 4: 1593–1616.

Hancock Financial Services. 2002. "Insight into Participant Investment Knowledge & Behavior."

JP Morgan. 2011. "Searching for Certainty."

CHAPTER 7

INVESTMENT SOLUTIONS PYRAMID

PREVIEW

One of the oft-cited benefits of 401(k) plans is the opportunity it gives plan participants to personally control their retirement savings. With this opportunity comes responsibility, namely, to construct a well-diversified portfolio that is appropriate for a long investment horizon. This is a complex task, even for financially literate people.

We recognize that the appetite for active engagement in portfolio selection among plan participants varies considerably: some have little or none, while others may be said to hunger to be actively involved. The behavioral solution to the challenges associated with constructing a well-diversified portfolio is a two-step system. The first takes account of participants' different appetites for active engagement in portfolio management and groups them into three categories: delegators, fine-tuners, and customizers. This is the Investment Appetite Pyramid. The second step in the system is to construct behavioral solutions that are appropriate for each of the three categories. This is the Investment Solutions Pyramid.

The bulk of the Investment Appetite Pyramid, 90 percent of workers, have no appetite for active involvement, and would prefer the responsibility to be shouldered by professionals. These are the delegators. The next tier, 9 percent or so of the total population, definitely want to be involved, but not deeply so. These are the fine-tuners. The third tier, the final 1 percent of the population, are extremely financially literate (for example, a company CFO and like-minded individuals), and wish to be extensively involved in the process. These are the customizers.

The Investment Solutions Pyramid is constructed as follows: The behavioral solution for delegators is the by-now familiar adoption of a simple, powerful default option: in this case it is to be invested in a professionally managed, one-stop solution, such as a target-date fund or managed account. Those who opt out of the default—the fine-tuners and the customizers—have solutions appropriate to their challenges and abilities. Fine-tuners would build their portfolios by selecting from a menu of funds that include, in addition to the target-date funds, five to nine core funds that comprise the building blocks of their portfolios. We also discuss the appropriate ordering within the menu of funds. Customizers would have a much broader menu of investments from which to choose, including a selection of specialty funds.

THE INVESTMENT APPETITE PYRAMID

Defined contribution retirement plans, such as 401(k) plans, offer participants the opportunity to select an investment portfolio that matches their tastes and their appetite for risk, given some target wealth accumulation at retirement. This opportunity is often cited as one of the benefits of defined contribution plans over traditional retirement vehicles. With this opportunity comes responsibility, of course, because the goal for individuals must be to end up with a well-diversified portfolio in line with their tastes and appetite for risk. This is not an easy task. The challenge, then, is to find the most effective—and easy—way for individuals to achieve that goal.

We recognize at the outset that there are differing levels of financial literacy and interest in investing among workers, different levels of appetite for being one's own portfolio manager. For this reason, unlike the simple (and powerful) solutions to the challenges of enrolling and saving, there will be multiple solutions to the challenge of investing wisely, in response to these different levels of appetite. The introduction to this section outlined the notion that some 90 percent of plan participants either lack the knowledge or the desire, or both, to be their own portfolio manager. They have no appetite for being actively involved in building their own portfolio, and would prefer to delegate the responsibility of that task to a professional. These "delegators" form the substantial base, or first tier, of what we call the Investment Appetite Pyramid.

The remaining 10 percent of the population, the top of the pyramid, would like to have some input into investment decisions. But even here, the appetite for investing differs. Most of this group, roughly 9 percent of the total population, would like a moderate degree of choice over what goes into their portfolios. They see themselves as relatively literate in the realm of finance, though far from being experts, and believe they can do a good-enough job of portfolio construction, as long as the investment options are not too challenging. We call this second tier of the pyramid the "fine-tuners," who have a moderate appetite for investing. The very tip of the pyramid, representing perhaps just 1 percent of the total population, are people such as the CFO and the like, who do indeed have extensive knowledge of investing. We call this third tier of the pyramid the "customizers." They have the most appetite of all for the task of portfolio construction.

Here's an analogy for our three types of investors. You are going to buy a new house. How do you go about it? If you are a delegator, you are satisfied with what the architect, the structural engineer, and the builder have constructed. You are content to turn the key, walk right in, and make sure the fridge is adequately stocked with beer. If you are a fine-tuner, on the other hand, you will probably want, for instance, to completely remodel the kitchen to your more demanding specifications. You think of yourself as something of a gourmet cook, after all. The customizer will have none of this, of course. He or she will want to be in on every detail of the design and construction from the beginning, having a clear vision of what the house should look like, and making sure the outcome is correct, right down to the design of the dog door.

Three levels of interest in the outcome, three levels of engagement in the building process. In the same way, three levels of appetite for constructing a portfolio lead to three levels of engagement in the process. Figure 7-1 shows the Investment Appetite Pyramid:

—————————————— The Investment Appetite Pyramid ——————————————

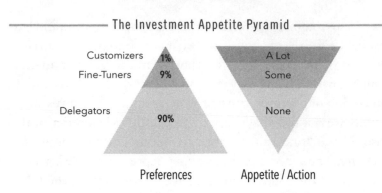

Figure 7-1. The first tier of the pyramid represents the 90 percent of plan participants who have little or no appetite for managing their own portfolio, the delegators. The second tier, 9 percent of the total, have a moderate appetite for portfolio construction, the fine-tuners. The third tier, just 1 percent of the population, are hungry for extensive control over their portfolios, the customizers.

Construction of the Investment Appetite Pyramid is the first of two steps to reaching a behavioral solution to the challenge of designing a well-diversified portfolio for all plan participants. The following pages describe the different behavioral challenges delegators, fine-tuners, and customizers face in getting what they need, and three tailored behavioral solutions to help them get there. This process will lead us to the Investment Solutions Pyramid, which is the second step to reaching a behavioral solution for all. We will see that little or no appetite for investing calls for minimal action (or none at all), a moderate appetite requires a moderate degree of action, and a greater appetite is satisfied only by considerable action.

THE CHALLENGES FOR THE DELEGATORS

We saw in the introduction to this section that 80 to 90 percent of plan participants have no desire to be their own portfolio manager, and really aren't sufficiently knowledgeable to do the task anyway. Recall that in one survey, 79 percent of participants believed that

a target-date fund would be a good solution for them (JP Mor
gan, 2011); and in another survey, 92 percent did not know what
constitutes a money market fund (Hancock, 2002). We also saw
from a research study that 80 percent of participants who had
opted to select their own portfolios judged them to be either
inferior to (61 percent) or about the same as (19 percent) a customized, professionally managed portfolio (Benartzi and Thaler, 2002).

Most people spend an alarmingly short amount of time planning for retirement, given how momentous a decision it is. One
study found that 58 percent of participants spend less than an
hour on all the decisions around retirement planning: deciding
whether to join, how much to save, how to invest, and who the
beneficiary should be (Benartzi and Thaler, 1999). A more recent
study puts this decision in the context of other decisions people
make in their daily lives (Benartzi, 2010). A survey of plan participants served by T. Rowe Price showed that around a quarter
of subjects spent as much time selecting a movie or a restaurant
as they did on planning their retirement; 30 percent spent at
least as much time choosing a book; the numbers for planning a
vacation or buying a car were 90 and 94 percent respectively in
comparison to planning for retirement.

Planning a successful vacation does indeed require some
planning, for example, looking through travel brochures or,
more likely, surfing the Web to find great deals. But the vacation
comes and goes in just a couple of weeks. Yet almost everyone
spends as much time planning for those two weeks in their life
as they do making decisions for the several decades they are
likely to spend in retirement. And a quarter of people spend the
same time selecting a movie or a restaurant, which activity is
likely to spread over a couple of hours, as they do on their retirement decisions. This is especially disturbing because retirement
planning is one of the most important financial decisions most

people make in their lives. And because of inertia, most partici-pants will never revisit their rushed and perhaps impulsive choices (Samuelson and Zeckhauser, 1988).

It hardly seems necessary to reiterate that most plan partici-pants should not be their own portfolio managers, but we will, in the interests of completing the picture. We do so in two realms. The first is in measures of performance, and the second is the matter of company stock.

In the first realm, a study of one million participants in one thousand retirement plans found that although plan sponsors offer efficient investment menus, many participants fail to con-struct efficient portfolios, which can lead to a reduction in retirement wealth by 20 percent because of participants' poor investment decisions (Tang et al., 2010). Similarly, a survey by Financial Engines finds that only one-third of 401(k) plan par-ticipants who manage their own accounts have appropriately diversified portfolios (Financial Engines, 2010). In both of these cases, plan participants' freedom to manage their own portfolios produced poorer outcomes than if they had gone with a profes-sionally managed, default alternative.

This conclusion is also supported by further studies of the performance of individual investors. For instance, in the twenty years ending in 2010, the average equity investor in the United States had an average annual return of 3.8 percent, compared with 9.14 percent for the S&P 500 (Dalbar, 2011). And several studies by Terrence Odean and colleagues show that individual investors, on average, pay a "penalty" of 2 to 4 percentage points on their annual returns through overconfidence, trading at the wrong time, and buying the wrong stocks (Barber and Odean, 2000; Barber and Odean, 2008; Barber et al., 2009).

One investment that is favored by many participants, when available, is company stock. In the 2002 Hancock survey, respondents rated company stock the category of investments about which they were most knowledgeable. However, their professed judgment about it was alarming at best. For instance, asked to rate its risk compared with other investments, respondents put it lower than diversified stock funds. To put this in perspective, the respondents' confidence in company stock (their own) was robust, despite having recently seen employees at Enron and WorldCom lose most of their retirement savings through having the same confidence in their company's stock.

There are several problems around investing retirement accounts in company stock (Benartzi et al., 2007). The first is that, as professionals know very well, owning a single security carries greater risk than a diversified portfolio, such as a mutual fund. Because of those risks, a dollar in company stock is worth barely fifty cents in a mutual fund (Meulbroek, 2002). The second problem, alluded to earlier, is that participants with a significant proportion of their retirement account invested in company stock run the risk of simultaneously losing their job *and* a substantial part of their retirement wealth.

Despite these well-known problems and very real risks, many employees continue to profess not only knowledge of, but also confidence in, company stock. And many enthusiastically put too much of their retirement funds where their misplaced confidence is: at the turn of the millennium, 11 million plan participants had more than 20 percent of their retirement assets in company stock, and five million committed more than 60 percent to it (Mitchell and Utkus, 2004). Clearly, the so-called halo effect of company stock blinds many plan participants to these dangers.

The paper in which Richard Thaler and I published our findings on participants' satisfaction with their own portfolio choices (mentioned earlier) was titled: "How Much Is Investor Autonomy Worth?" We answered our own question as follows: "Investor autonomy is not worth much," a conclusion that is supported by the various surveys and academic papers presented here.

DELEGATORS' SOLUTION: AUTO-INVEST

We have seen, therefore, that a large proportion of people have little or no appetite to be engaged investors, and many of those who do want to take their retirement futures in their own hands don't do a very good job at it. Given the complex nature of constructing a well-diversified portfolio, this widespread failure should not be surprising. The most effective and easy solution to that challenge, therefore, is to go with what most people want and is in their best interests: Auto-Invest.

By this we mean that, in addition to automatic enrollment in a plan (Auto-Takeoff), and automatic enrollment in a savings escalator (Auto-Climb), most employees would be best served by being automatically placed in a one-stop, professionally managed investment vehicle, such as a target-date fund or a managed account. In our Retirement Plane analogy, we refer to Auto-Invest as being on "Auto-Smooth," which ensures that the journey toward retirement wealth accumulation will be as safe and steady as possible. The alternative, managing one's own portfolio without the knowledge to do so skillfully, is what we call being on "Auto-Turbulent." This unwise path for financially naïve participants is, as we've seen, likely to lead to a very rough ride financially and, in some cases, even devastating results. Auto-Smooth provides greater diversification and financial security: participants have a well-diversified portfolio, and don't face the agony of choice or the anxiety over whether or not they have made the right decisions.

Having automatic enrollment in an investment vehicle chosen by the plan sponsor is not novel in itself, of course. This has been the choice architecture in many plans for many years, but the default option has typically been very conservative, often a money market fund (Madrian and Shea, 2001). The expectation was that over time plan participants would select investments that are more appropriate for long-term wealth accumulation. But, as Madrian and Shea demonstrated, because of inertia, most people remain in the conservative default investment option. The default option we are recommending here, be it a target-date fund or similar investment vehicle, puts participants in the appropriate investment vehicle from the start—and because of inertia, most people will stay there. In this case, inertia is working in participants' best interests, which is to be in a one-stop, professionally managed fund.

As with all the default options around retirement planning, participants are free to opt out of the default investment option at any time. We have seen in the present context that most people will happily accept and stay with the default option, but some, as we indicated at the beginning of the chapter, have an appetite for investing, and will want to be actively engaged in building their own portfolios. These are the fine-tuners and the customizers.

THE CHALLENGES FOR THE FINE-TUNERS

We've noted that selecting a well-diversified portfolio is a complex task, and not just in the number and diversity of options available. Fine-tuners also face behavioral challenges in making wise selections from the options on offer, challenges that may stem principally from the manner in which those options are offered.

When people face difficult choice options, they often sensibly resort to rules of thumb. One simple example is to divide contributions equally among a small number of investment options, as we saw Harry Markowitz do in the introductory chapter. This rule of thumb has been called the 1/n rule (Benartzi and Thaler, 2001). Although following this rule of thumb doesn't lead to potentially disastrous outcomes, as being heavily invested in company stock may, it is nevertheless what we call "naïve diversification." It doesn't lead to optimal solutions. Following are the most important challenges that might, unwittingly, lead fine-tuners into choices that might not be rational or wise. Some of these behavioral challenges are quite counterintuitive:

Choice overload. It has been commonly assumed in economics that more choice is a good thing for the consumer, and certainly not a negative. From classic theories of free enterprise to supermarket shelves that offer seemingly endless varieties of potato chips and soft drinks, the desire for infinite choice pervades our culture. However, there is a growing body of research in psychology and economics (from laboratory experiments and real-world observations) indicating that there is such a thing as too much choice. Specifically, people find it easier to make decisions when faced with a small menu of options than with many possible choices. Anyone who has faced row upon row of myriad cereal choices in a supermarket aisle understands this very well: a large array of choices can simply be overwhelming. This has been called choice overload, a phenomenon that Sheena Iyengar has studied extensively (Iyengar, 2011).

Here is a simple experiment that shows that increasing the number of choices can be appealing at first, but that very soon choice overload kicks in. It involves the proportion of subjects who were willing to buy pens when the choice of different pens on offer increased from two to twenty. The researchers, Avni Shah and George Wolford, found that as the number of pens on offer grew from two to ten, subjects' willingness to buy initially increased. When the range of choices expanded beyond ten,

———— Degree of Choice and Percentage of Subjects Buying a Pen ————

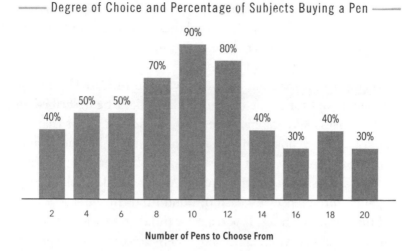

Number of Pens to Choose From

Figure 7-2. As the number of choices of pens on offer increased, the percentage of subjects buying them also increased, but only up to a total of ten choices. After that choice overload kicked in and subjects became more reluctant to buy. (Source: Avni M. Shah and George Wolford, *Psychological Science*, Vol. 18, Issue 5, pp. 369-370, copyright © 2007 by Association for Psychological Science. (Reprinted by Permission of SAGE Publications.)

however, the proportion of subjects who were willing to buy dropped, and quite dramatically so after twelve. Simple experiment, nice result. (See Figure 7-2.)

Iyengar and colleagues have demonstrated choice overload in the realm of investment options in retirement plans. Specifically, they found that when the number of funds offered in a 401(k) plan increases beyond a very small number, enrollment in the plan begins to fall. For every ten new options offered, enrollment drops by between 1.5 and 2 percent (Iyengar et al., 2004). And for employees who do join the plan, for every ten more funds offered in the plan's menu, participants reduced their exposure to equities by 3.28 percent (Iyengar and Kamenica, 2010). The authors speculate that as the number of equity funds in the menu increased, so too did the proportion of specialty funds (such as energy, health care, precious metals, and mining, for example). They further suggest that some participants found these specialty funds intimidating, and opted instead to take shelter in "psychologically safer" bond funds or money market funds.

An alternative explanation is that when intimidated by a long list, people opt for a rule of thumb that might be described as "go for what is psychologically easiest." Research shows that, in this case, the psychologically easiest choice might be what is first on the list. Typically, what is first on a list of investment options is also the most conservative option, which would explain participants' "preference" for cash or bond funds in the study.

The primacy effect. If you are a candidate for elected office you should do all you legally can to ensure that your name is first, or at least very high up, on the ballot. Change your name to Jon Aardvark if necessary, wherever election forms are printed alphabetically. The reason is that position in a list of options (a ballot in this case) matters a lot. (Some states rotate names, so Jon Aardvark might have to find some other means of getting elected.) Research shows that candidates listed first on a ballot enjoy at least a 2 percent advantage in the polls, and in political elections 2 percent can be the difference between being an "in" and looking for some other line of work (Koppell and Steen, 2004; Krosnick et al., 2004).

The German psychologist Herman Ebbinghaus recognized the importance of position on a list of options a century ago in something he called the "serial position effect." In this case, where first position holds sway, it is known as "primacy," as alluded to earlier. Primacy has been observed at work in many situations, including people looking for car repair services in the Yellow Pages (AAA Automotive Repair would be a good company name to have) (Lohse, 1997) and in marketing (see, for example, Buda and Zhang, 2000). And, a favorite, in wine tasting (Mantonakis et al., 2009).

In this study, undergraduates and people from the local community (in Ontario, Canada) were given between two and five glasses of local wine, and were asked to note down their preference. In every case, tasters displayed a strong preference for the first glass of wine in the tasting series. What the tasters did not know was that within each tasting series, the glasses of wine were identical, not different, as the tasters had been led to believe. Most of the tasters weren't enologically sophisticated, but some did declare a good deal of experience with tasting wine. It is therefore especially amusing that those who professed most knowledge of wines displayed an even stronger primacy effect than naïve tasters. Primacy triumphs over taste buds and experience!

Less amusing than the wine buffs' inability to know what they were drinking is the potential effect that primacy might wield when plan participants are offered a list of funds to choose from in building their portfolios. If riskier investments are at or near the top of the menu, participants might unwittingly select a much more aggressive portfolio than is suitable for their tastes, for instance. It is, however, not uncommon to see investments listed from the least to the most risky, or sometimes alphabetically. Whatever the case, the research on primacy tells us that how investments are listed could affect what is selected. Research also shows that with long lists, a second, related effect kicks in: recency. With long lists, many people find that the final items stay in their mind almost as tenaciously as the first items. With long lists, therefore, those at the beginning and those at the end will be picked more often than those in the middle, with primacy often being the stronger effect.

The bottom line of these various behavioral challenges that the fine-tuners will face in building a well-balanced portfolio is stark: the choice architecture around the investment options offered to them can have an unusually strong influence on what those portfolios will contain. Plan sponsors therefore bear a heavy responsibility to ensure that participants are not unwittingly guided to investment decisions that are not necessarily in their best interests.

FINE-TUNERS' SOLUTIONS: THE MAGICAL NUMBER 7, AND EASY FIRST

The goal of the behavioral solutions to the above behavioral challenges is to help plan sponsors and their advisers ensure that fine-tuners make smart investment decisions.

The first question is "How many funds should be in the menu?" We've seen that as a choice menu enlarges, people's decisions can be skewed in counterintuitive ways: a large menu may cause participants to shy away from equities and gravitate to simpler, easier-to-understand bonds or equivalent securities; or maybe to opt for the psychologically easy choice, which is to select options from the top of the list. Decades ago, most plans offered two or perhaps three options: a cash or stable-value fund, a stock fund, and (in large companies) company stock. By the turn of the millennium the average number of funds had grown to eleven. A decade later that number had virtually doubled, to an average of eighteen in 2010 (PSCA, 2011). But is eighteen the "right" number?

In a classic paper published half a century ago, Harvard psychologist George A. Miller mused on what he called "the magical number seven," a number that pervades human lives in many ways (Miller, 1956). "What about the seven wonders of the world," he wrote, "the seven seas, the seven deadly sins, the seven daughters of Atlas in the Pleiades, the seven ages of man, the seven levels of hell, the seven primary colors, the seven notes of the musical scale, and the seven days of the week? What about the seven-point rating scale, the seven categories for absolute judgment, the seven objects in the span of attention, and the seven digits in the span of immediate memory?"

There is, Miller suggested, something about human cognition that limits our ability to handle information of all kinds so that we gravitate naturally to the number seven (plus or minus two) when making sense of the world. We are simply wired that way, Miller suggested. Having eighteen investment options in a 401(k) plan is therefore probably too many. To make the selection process as easy as possible for plan participants, we suggest that plan sponsors would be wise to go down this well-trodden psychological path, and aim to offer an investment menu of seven (plus or minus two) options. A consensus of experts recently surveyed by the TIAA-CREF Institute put the appropriate number of funds in a menu at between five and ten (TIAA-CREF, 2011).

In addition to target-date funds offered to delegators, the menu of portfolio building blocks for fine-tuners might include cash, bonds, large-cap and small-cap stock funds, international stock funds, and Treasury Inflation-Protected Securities, with the latter often receiving too little weight in target-date funds Larger employers that have company stock should limit participants' exposure to no more than, say, 10 percent and consider the Sell More Tomorrow program that Richard Thaler and I developed. That program calls for gradual divesting of excessive company stock holdings, down to the target level of 10 percent of portfolio assets. It offers the behavioral benefit of not worrying about selling it all at the wrong time, and it also offers the economic benefit of not driving the company share price down by selling all at once. More details on the program are available in Benartzi and Thaler, 2003.

It is not our place here to be specific about the exact makeup of the investment menu. Plans sponsors should work closely with their financial advisers to draw up an investment policy statement and select a menu of core funds that matches the principles set out in the statement.

Plan sponsors and their advisers obviously carry a great responsibility for the composition of participants' portfolios, in two ways. First, they must decide which funds to include in the investment menu. And second, they must decide how that menu is structured, given the behavioral challenges described in the previous section. They should be aware that there is no neutral way that a list of options is offered, and they should be diligent in avoiding unwittingly emphasizing an asset class that does not merit such exposure by, for instance, placing it first on the list. The top of the menu should be occupied by funds that are most appropriate for the widest range of participants. We call this choice architecture "Easy First." It is akin to displaying food in a school cafeteria so that children see the salads before they get to the burgers. Result: they will eat more salad and fewer burgers. Simple. And powerful. In both cases.

Those relatively few plan participants who are in the third tier of the pyramid—the financially sophisticated customizers— have an appetite for a menu that includes more specialty investments. These might include sector funds, such as biotech or health care, or geographically specific international funds, such as an Asia fund, or perhaps an emerging markets fund. Customizers have sufficient knowledge and skill in this arena to be able to take care of themselves.

THE INVESTMENT SOLUTIONS PYRAMID

The behavioral solutions just described for fine-tuners and customizers complete what might be called the Investment Solutions Pyramid:

The solution for delegators is **Auto-Invest**.
For fine-tuners it is the **Magical Number 7** and **Easy
    First**.
And for customizers it is **Build It Yourself**.

There is a direct relationship between the Investment Appetite Pyramid and the Investment Solutions Pyramid. Delegators, who have no appetite for active engagement in portfolio
construction, are required to take no action. For fine-tuners,
with their moderate appetite for engagement, the solution
requires them to take more action and to make a selection from
a menu of around five to nine core funds. The highly developed
appetite for engagement among customizers ensures very active
engagement, navigating an investment landscape that is quite
complex and challenging. As appetite for engagement in portfolio formation increases, so, too, does the number of actions that
make up the behavioral solution in each tier, as we can see in the
Investment Solutions Pyramid:

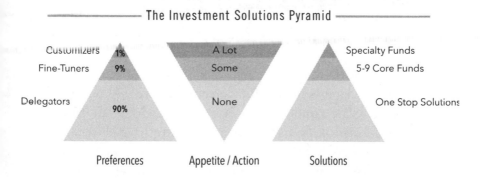

The Investment Solutions Pyramid

Customizers	1%	A Lot	Specialty Funds
Fine-Tuners	9%	Some	5-9 Core Funds
Delegators	90%	None	One Stop Solutions

Preferences   Appetite / Action   Solutions

Figure 7-3. The solution for those with little appetite for being actively engaged in managing their own portfolios, the delegators, is very simple: automatic enrollment in a one-
stop investment solution, such as a target-date fund. Fine-tuners, who have a moderate
investment appetite, have to make a selection from around a menu of five to nine core
funds. The solution for customizers, with their extensive appetite, is a much broader
menu of investment options, including specialty funds.

And at each level the bucket of investments offered is different: for the delegators it is a one-stop, professionally managed, well-diversified investment solution, such as a target-date fund or managed account; the selection for fine-tuners includes seven (plus or minus two) core funds; the investment choice landscape for customizers is much broader and varied, and includes an array of specialty funds not found in the other two buckets.

Plan sponsors and advisers who construct an Investment Solutions Pyramid in the manner just described are being good choice architects, working in the best interests of employees.

COUNTERARGUMENTS

My target-date fund performed very poorly over the past couple of years, and yet you are telling me that 90 percent of participants should be invested solely in them?

There has been great variation in the performance of target-date funds. For instance, in a survey of thirty-five 2010 target-date funds from thirty-five major vendors, most of the funds lost between 20 and 30 percent in 2008, but one lost 41.2 percent—a disaster for workers two years from retirement. But many lost 20 percent or less, and one recorded a loss of only 9.1 percent.* It isn't the concept of target-date funds that is a problem with your fund's performance. Perhaps you happened to have chosen one with excessive exposure to risk. It is therefore critical that you work with your financial adviser to select a well-diversified target-date fund.

---

* Data provided by James Macey, Allianz Global Investors–U.S., October 2011.

I currently have twenty-three funds in my plan, and you are suggesting I have no more than seven or so. Am I supposed to fire the other sixteen?

No, you don't have to fire them. You can reposition them elsewhere in the Action Pyramid, in the third tier for the customizers, for example.

If I arrange the fund menu so that plan participants will invest "appropriately," will I be perceived as giving investment advice? Might I be "tricking" plan participants into investing more aggressively than they really want to?

Because there is no neutral design of a list—in this case, an investment menu—you can't avoid giving implicit advice. And if you are already providing implicit guidance, you might as well provide good advice and not bad advice. You aren't trying to have participants invest aggressively or conservatively. Instead, you are just guiding them in the right direction so that they end up with well-diversified portfolios. Thus, at the top of the menu should be the fund that is appropriate for the widest range of participants, which we call Easy First. Work with your adviser to ensure that participants end up with a well-diversified portfolio through their selections.

Shouldn't I have a relatively long list of funds from which participants can choose, to make sure I have at least some good ones in there?

This blockbuster approach is not a good idea, not least because you risk triggering choice overload among your participating employees. But the real issue is that you should be working with an adviser who you are confident can suggest a collection of investment building blocks that will lead to well-diversified portfolios. If you don't have confidence in your current menu of funds, you need to discuss it with your adviser (or find a better one).

My plan provider isn't able, or willing, to offer the three-tiered structure you are proposing, either on the enrollment form or the Web site.

Our response to this is, as always, that you should consider finding a new plan provider who is BeFi capable, in the best interests of your employees.

BEHAVIORAL FINANCE ACTIONS

▶**Action 1:** Implement Auto-Invest for all participants, which puts them into a target-date fund, a managed account service, or other one-stop solutions. This could serve about 90 percent of the participants. This is the first tier of the Investment Appetite Pyramid, the delegators. Around 10 percent will opt out.

▶**Action 2:** Work with your financial adviser to create a menu that, in addition to the target-date funds, offers from five to nine core funds, which are the building blocks for a well-diversified portfolio. At the top of the menu should be the fund that is appropriate for the widest range of participants, or Easy First. Most of the participants who opt out of the default option (9 percent of the total) will find this degree of engagement in portfolio management attractive. This is the second tier of the Investment Appetite Pyramid, the fine-tuners.

▶**Action 3:** For the customizers, the 1 percent of participants who are financially sophisticated and don't find the second tier option attractive, expand the menu with an array of specialty funds. This will satisfy the third tier's appetite for more sophisticated investing.

▶**Action 4:** For plan sponsors who offer company stock to employees, ensure that there is an upper limit of 10 percent in individuals' accounts.

REFERENCES

Barber, Brad M., and Terrence Odean. 2000. "Trading Is Hazardous to Your Wealth: The Common Stock Investment Performance of Individual Investors." *The Journal of Finance* 55, no. 2: 773–806.

———. 2008. "All That Glitters: The Effect of Attention and News on the Buying Behavior of Individual and Institutional Investors." *The Review of Financial Studies* 21, no. 2: 785–818.

Barber, Brad M., Yi-Tsung Lee, Yu-Jane Liu, and Terrance Odean. "Just How Much Do Individual Investors Lose by Trading?" *The Review of Financial Studies* 22, no. 2: 609–32.

Benartzi, Shlomo. 2001. "Excessive Extrapolation and the Allocation of 401(k) Accounts to Company Stock?" *Journal of Finance* 56, no 5, pp. 1747–64.

———. 2010. "Time (mis)Allocation and Retirement Funds." *401(k)Now* (Winter).

Benartzi, Shlomo, and Richard H. Thaler. 1999. "Risk Aversion or Myopia? Choices in Repeated Gambles and Retirement Investments." *Management Science* 45, no. 3: 364–81.

———. 2001. "Naïve Diversification Strategies in Defined Contribution Saving Plans." *American Economic Review* 91: 79–98.

———. 2002. "How Much Is Investor Autonomy Worth?" *The Journal of Finance* 57, no. 4: 1593–1616.

———. 2003. "Using Behavioral Economics to Improve Diversification in 401(k) Plans: Solving the Company Stock Problem." Working paper, UCLA.

Benartzi, Shlomo, Richard H. Thaler, Stephen P. Utkus, and Cass Sunstein. 2007. "Company Stock, Market Rationality, and Legal Reform." *Journal of Law and Economics* 50, no. 1: 45–79.

Buda, Richard, and Yong Zhang. 2000. "Consumer Product Evaluation: The Interactive Effect of Message Framing, Presentation Order, and Source Credibility." *Journal of Product and Brand Management* 9, no. 4: 229–42.

Financial Engines. 2010. "The Financial Engines National 401(k) Evaluation."

Hancock Financial Services. 2002. "Insight into Participant Investment Knowledge and Behavior."

Hancock Financial Services. 2007. "Outcomes of Participant Investment Strategies, 1997–2006."

Iyengar, Sheena. 2011. *The Art of Choosing.* Abacus Books.

Iyengar, Sheena S., G. Huberman, and W. Jiang. 2004. "How Much Choice Is Too Much: Determinants of Individual Contributions in 401K Retirement Plans." In *Pension Design and Structure: New Lessons from Behavioral Finance,* edited by Olivia S. Mitchell and Stephen P. Utkus. Oxford University Press.

Iyengar, Sheena S., and Emir Kamenica. 2010. "Choice Proliferation, Simplicity Seeking, and Asset Allocation." *Journal of Public Economics* 94, no. 7/8: 530–39.

Lohse, Gerald. 1997. "Consumer Eye Movement Patterns on Yellow Pages Advertizing." *Journal of Advertising* 26, no. 1: 61–73.

Madrian, Brigitte C., and Dennis F. Shea. 2001. "The Power of Suggestion: Inertia in 401(k) Participation and Savings Behavior." *The Quarterly Journal of Economics* 116, no. 4: 1149–87.

Mantonakis, Antonia, Pauline Rodero, Isabelle Lesschaeve, and Reid Hastie. 2009. "Order in Choice: Effects of Serial Position on Preferences." *Psychological Science* 20, no. 1: 1309–12.

Meulbroek, Lisa K. 2002. "Company Stock in Pension Plans: How Costly Is It?" *Journal of Law and Economics* 48, no. 2: 443–74.

Miller, George A. 1956. "The Magical Number Seven, Plus or Minus Two: Some Limits on Our Capacity for Processing Information." *Psychological Review* 63: 81–95.

Mitchell, Olivia S., and Stephen P. Utkus. 2004. "The Role of Company Stock in Defined Contribution Plans," in *The Pension Challenge: Risk Transfers and Retirement Income Security,* edited by Olivia Mitchell and Kent Smetters. Oxford University Press.

JP Morgan. 2011. "Searching for Certainty."

PSCA. 2011. "54th Annual Survey."

Samuelson, W., and R. Zeckhauser. 1988. "Status Quo Bias in Decision Making." *Journal of Risk and Uncertainty* 1: 1–79.

Shah, Avni M., and George Wolford. 2007. "Buying Behavior as a Function of Parametric Variation of Number of Choices." *Psychological Science* 18: 369–70.

Tang, Ning, Olivia S. Mitchell, Gary R. Mottola, and Stephen P. Utkus. 2010. "The Efficiency of Sponsor and Participant Portfolio Choices in 401(k) Plans," IRM WP2009-14 Insurance and Risk Management Working Paper.

Thaler, Richard H., and Cass R. Sunstein. 2009. *Nudge: Improving Decisions about Health, Wealth, and Happiness.* New York: Penguin Books.

TIAA-CREF. 2011. "Rethinking Defined Contribution Plan Design: A Survey of Experts." *Trends and Issues* (August).

CHAPTER 8

THE LIFETIME STATEMENT

PREVIEW

The appropriate investment horizon for most plan participants is long term because the great majority of them have decades of saving and investing ahead of them. Nevertheless, the quarterly statements that plan sponsors are required by law to provide participants typically emphasize a short investment horizon, namely, the previous quarter's returns. The quarterly return is sometimes the only performance information present on the first page of the statement. In these cases year-to-date returns follow on a later page, while longer-term information, such as data for the life of the account, appears subsequently, if at all.

Behavioral finance research shows that plan participants are subject to what has been called myopic loss aversion, a combination of loss aversion and a focus on the short term. When subjects in a laboratory experiment are shown short-term performance data for stocks and bonds, they elect to invest disproportionately in bonds. Viewing long-term performance data of the same historical returns has the opposite effect: subjects favor investment in stocks.

The actual asset allocation of people in one experiment (faculty at the University of Southern California) was almost identical to the asset allocation obtained when they saw short-term performance data in the experiment. Although other interpretations are possible, this observation implies that presenting quarterly return information prominently on quarterly statements, as is typically the case, might cause plan participants to become myopic investors. Myopic investors tend to invest more conservatively in down markets and more aggressively in up markets than is wise over the long term. Because of loss aversion, myopic investors also suffer more mental anguish when quarterly statements highlight and focus on short-term losses.

We propose renaming the quarterly statement to reflect the long time horizon that is appropriate for retirement accounts. The new name is Lifetime Statement. This is not just a labeling exercise; it is a new way of thinking about the information provided to plan participants. Lifetime Statements would present longer-term performance information up front, with quarterly returns coming later. This renaming and restructuring of quarterly statements would encourage plan participants to take a long-term strategy in choosing investments, and it would help avoid lost sleep over short-term losses, which are inevitable even in rising markets. The adoption of Lifetime Statements to replace the traditional quarterly statements is an example of changing the information architecture in the best interests of employees.

WHAT IS THE CORRECT TIME HORIZON
FOR ACCOUNT INFORMATION?

The previous chapter demonstrated that one important factor in assembling a sound retirement portfolio is the manner in which *choice* is presented. For example, we saw that when presented with a list of investment options, plan participants might disproportionally select those at the top of the list. In this chapter the manner in which *information* is presented, and its influence on people's decisions, is our single, primary focus. Our question therefore is twofold:

- In what manner is account performance information currently presented to individual participants?
- What impact does this manner of presentation have on participants' investment behavior, if any?

Every three months plan participants receive in their mailboxes a statement of their accounts' performance. (The information is also available on the plan's Web sites.) We surveyed a sample of quarterly statements and found a good deal of variability in the length (ranging from two to six pages) and how the information is presented. There was, however, one thing common to virtually all of them: the previous quarter's performance appears on page one, prominently displayed. It is designed to catch the attention, and it does. The Pension Protection Act of 2006 requires sponsors of defined contribution plans to provide participants with a "pension benefit statement . . . at least each calendar quarter." Neither we nor our ERISA attorneys can find language that says providing the previous quarter's *performance* is mandatory. Nevertheless, there seems to have been an assumption in the industry that the quarterly statement should not only include the previous quarter's performance, but also that it should be prominently displayed. The practice has unfortunately become ubiquitous.

Here is what the first page of quarterly statements often conveys:

- Beginning balance
- Ending balance
- Rate of return:
  - **This period**
  - **Year to date**

Where the first page includes information in addition to the quarterly return, the figure for the quarterly return is typically the most prominent item. Later pages display information on asset allocation, details of the performance of funds in the account, how future contributions will be allocated, and so on. Long-term information, such as how well individuals' accounts have performed since they enrolled in the plan, is difficult to find or even absent.

Now consider this. New hires who enroll in their company's 401(k) plan early on, in their thirties, say, have three decades of saving and investing in front of them, and some decades in retirement. The average plan participant (in his or her mid-forties) is also in a world where the proper measure is in decades. The same goes for the majority of plan participants. The correct time horizon over which participants should be evaluating their retirement accounts, therefore, is the long term. Short-term performance should be of limited concern because short-term moves in the markets typically do not predict long-term outcomes.

In general, therefore, there is a striking mismatch between the information that is most important to participants (the long-term performance) and the figure that is most prominent in quarterly statements (the quarterly performance). Roughly three-quarters of plan participants open their quarterly statements; of those who look at the statement, 72 percent spend three minutes or less perusing them (Koster, 2009). The information that is prominently presented on page one inevitably looms large in the readers' minds; and given the typical brevity of participants' attention to the statement, many will not even get past the first page.

Our question here is this: what influence, if any, might this manner of presenting retirement account performance information have on participants' outlook as investors?

UNINTENDED CONSEQUENCES OF THE QUARTERLY STATEMENT

We approach this issue by means of a hypothetical bet that is based on one that economist Paul Samuelson made famous in the literature almost half a century ago. How would you feel about a bet that offers a "tails you win $200, heads you lose $100"? Would you accept the bet? If you are like most people, you would turn it down, because of loss aversion. That loss of $100 looms large in your mind, despite the potential of a sizeable win. Now suppose you are offered that same bet twice in succession. What is your response now? You might well be scratching your head and thinking: "What, is he nuts? Why would I submit myself to doing something twice that I've already said is unpleasant enough once?" Again, like most people, you would turn down the bet.

Okay. Here's a third bet. This time you have a 25 percent chance of winning $400, a 50 percent chance of winning $100, and a 25 percent chance of losing $200. "Now you're talking," you might say, "this one looks a whole lot more attractive than anything you've offered before." You accept the bet, which, of course, is a very rational thing to do.

The point about bet three is that, although it does indeed "look a whole lot more attractive" than the other bets, it is in fact mathematically identical to bet number two. The difference between bets two and three is in the presentation. Bet two focuses on the short-term steps to the outcome, whereas bet three presents the aggregate outcome in a very attention-getting manner, the long-term view, if you will. A cartoon representation will help.

—— The Emotional Experience of Observing Short-term Losses ——

First Round	Second Round	Emotional Experience
+ $200	+ $200	☺
+ $200	- $100	☹
- $100	+ $200	☹
- $100	- $100	☹

Figure 8-1. Evaluating the bet at each stage lays open the possibility that myopic loss aversion will obscure the possible positive aggregate outcome.

Look at the first possible sequence of results in the figure:

► You win the first round, so you feel happy; and the second, too, so you are still happy at the end of the bet.

► In the second sequence you again win the first round, so you feel happy, but this time you lose the second round. Because of the intensity of loss aversion, the pleasure of your first win is swamped, and your overall experience of the two coin tosses is misery.

▶ You lose the first round in the third possible sequence of results. You feel miserable, and even the pleasure of winning the second round is insufficient to boost your spirits. You are still miserable.

▶ The fourth possible sequence of results is one anxiety after another, with one loss following on the other. You are definitely miserable.

The bottom line here is that when you evaluate the bet after each roll of the dice, loss aversion can kick in and make you feel miserable, even when the aggregate outcome is positive, as in the middle two sequences. This short-horizon view of the overall bet has a strong, negative impact on how you feel about the bet overall. This was how you reacted to being offered bet number two.

Now look at the very same possible sequences of results, but instead of checking the result after each coin toss to evaluate the bet you focus only on the aggregate outcome. Again, a cartoon representation helps.

——— The Emotional Experience of Ignoring Short-term Losses ———

First Round	Second Round	Total	Emotional Experience
?	?	+ $400	☺
?	?	+ $100	☺
?	?	+ $100	☺
?	?	**- $200**	☹

Figure 8-2. By focusing only on the aggregate outcome a player avoids being negatively influenced by myopic loss aversion.

Because you haven't checked on the results after each toss, you don't see any negative short-term outcomes on the way to the aggregate outcome. Same sequences of possible results as in the first condition, but when you look only at the aggregate outcomes, you are happy with three of the sequences of possible results rather than just one, as shown in the figure below. This was how you responded to bet number three. You definitely liked it.

By taking a long-horizon view of the bet, that is, monitoring only the aggregate outcome, you avoid myopic loss aversion and are better able to accurately evaluate the long-term worth of the bet.

This brings us to the matter at hand: what impact do different evaluation periods—short-term versus long-term—have on participants' behavior as investors?

To get an answer to this question, Thaler and I did an experiment with non-faculty staff members at the University of Southern California (USC). We asked them to say how they would allocate retirement savings between two funds, Fund A and Fund B, based on historical performance data we would give them. To avoid any bias that might arise through people's predisposition to favor either stocks or bonds, we didn't tell them that one was a stock fund and the other a bond fund. We wanted them to respond only to performance information.

We used performance information on stocks and five-year bonds over a sixty-eight-year period, 1926–1993, for Funds A and B, respectively. We framed the information in two ways: short-evaluation period and long-evaluation period. The short-horizon frame was the distribution of annual rates of return from the historic data, arranged from worst to best, for both Fund A and Fund B. We called this the One-Year view. This is equivalent to bet number two, when the results of the coin tosses are monitored one by one. We produced a distribution of thirty-year performances using the following simulation. We picked years at random from the 1926–1993 period, thirty times. This creates one possible thirty-year experience. Then we computed

——————— Worst- to Best-Case Outcomes for Stocks and Bonds ———————

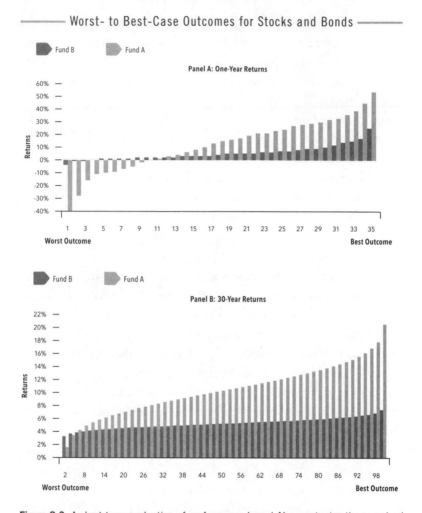

Figure 8-3. A short-term evaluation of performance (panel A) accentuates the perceived riskiness of stocks (fund A) compared with bonds (fund B). A long-term view (panel B) greatly reduces perceived riskiness of stocks, which are now seen as attractive investment prospects. (Source: Benartzi and Thaler, 1999. Reprinted by permission, Benartzi, S., R. H. Thaler, "Risk Aversion or Myopia? Choices in repeated gamble and retirement invest-ments." *Management Science*, 45(3), 1999, 364– 81. Copyright 1999, the Institute for Operations Research and the Management Sciences, 7240 Parkway Drive, Suite 300, Hanover, MD 21076.)

the average annual rate of return for this thirty-year period. This is done 10,000 times, computing an average annual rate of return each time, which we ranked from worst to best for both the stock fund and the bond fund. Each of these thirty-year averages is the equivalent to bet number three, where the aggregate outcome is prominently visible. (See Figure 8-3.)

What we have, therefore, is performance information for stocks and for bonds, each presented in two ways: one-year and Thirty-Year views of the same data set. When you compare the two charts in figure 8-3 you can see clearly that the one-year chart accentuates the perceived riskiness of investing in stocks. Over a one-year period, for example, the likelihood that stocks underperform bonds is about one-third, compared with just 5 percent over a thirty-year period. Given what we know about myopic loss aversion, we predicted that subjects who see the one-year chart would elect to invest less in stocks than those who see the thirty-year chart, because the likelihood of stocks experiencing a loss decreases as its horizon lengthens. The mean allocation to stocks by subjects who saw the one-year returns was 41 percent compared with twice that, 82 percent, for subjects who saw the thirty-year chart (Benartzi and Thaler, 1999).

This is a very strong laboratory result. But how does it measure up to the real world? In a separate study with USC faculty we found a higher allocation to the stock fund, 63 percent, by subjects who saw the short-term view, than in the first experiment. We attribute the greater bullishness for stocks among this group compared with the first group to their greater financial sophistication. Those faculty who saw the long-term view in this experiment allocated 83 percent of assets to stocks. When we asked these subjects what their *actual* allocation to stock funds was in their defined contribution plan we found it to be 66 percent, which is very similar to the short-view figure in the experiment, 63 percent. We knew that the vendor's statements emphasized short-term returns, as is typical.

What do these results tell us? One interpretation is that these faculty members respond to the short-term view of their quarterly statements with myopic loss aversion, making them myopic investors. This is precisely what we see with the short-term view in the experiment. The prominent placement of quarterly returns on page one of the quarterly statement was probably not intended to turn participants into myopic investors. That, however, appears to have been the unintended consequence.

There is a second possible interpretation of the investment choices of the USC faculty in their retirement accounts. If they believed that future return on equities would be lower than historic returns, then a conservative investment position would be warranted. This is what Thaler and I saw with the same pool of subjects with whom we ran the above experiment, but with an artificially reduced equity premium, 3 percent instead of the historic 6 percent. This manipulation clearly makes long-term investment in stocks far less attractive, with the result that time horizon had very little influence on subjects' asset allocation. In this case, average equity allocation under the One-Year view was 63 percent, just as it was with historic equity premium, while under the Thirty-Year view it was just 69 percent.

While bearing in mind the possibility that a conservative investment position might be a logical response to a more pessimistic outlook on future equity returns, the above research shows us that a short-term view of investment outcomes really does provoke myopic behavior in plan participants. Other researchers' findings support this position.

For instance, Thaler et al. (1997) observed similar results to those above with an experiment in which undergraduates were asked to imagine they were portfolio managers for a small college. They were presented with performance information for two funds, a stock fund and a bond fund, but, as in the above experiment, they were not told explicitly which was which. They responded only to the performance of the two funds, as in the earlier experiment. Some participants saw performance information at frequent intervals, and were able to make adjustments as they saw fit. Others saw performance information much less frequently, and therefore had fewer opportunities to change asset allocation over the same period of time as the first group. In other words, these were short- and long-term views, respectively, as in the previous experiments.

As with the earlier experiment, subjects who saw and acted on short-term information invested in bonds about twice as much as subjects who saw long-term information. In terms of financial outcomes, subjects who worked with short-term information significantly underperformed those who saw long-term information (Thaler et al., 1997). "The subjects in the monthly condition had more information and more freedom than the subjects in the [long-term] condition," note the authors, "but more is not always better." Providing performance information to plan participants in a short-term frame, note the authors, "is likely to encourage their worst tendencies." Gneezy and Potters (1997) and Gneezy et al. (2003) report very similar results.

University of Chicago economist John List has argued that experienced professionals are much less susceptible to the kinds of behavioral challenges described in this book (List, 2004). It is also true that the subjects recruited for some of the above experiments were undergraduates who were, for the most part, innocent of the world of finance. Professional traders might therefore be expected not to succumb to myopic loss aversion under the kind of experimental designs typically employed. As it turns out, innocence is apparently not a factor here. In an experiment with futures and options traders from the Chicago Board of Trade, with undergraduates as a control group, List and Michael S. Haigh found that the experienced professionals displayed a *greater* degree of myopic loss aversion than the undergraduates (Haigh and List, 2005).

Given that insight, it is not surprising that the decisions of plan sponsors are also influenced by myopic loss aversion. Studies show that they are very quick to replace fund managers whose short-term performance (one year, typically) is poor, with fund managers who have better short-term performance. However, the future performance of the new fund is typically no better, and often worse, than the dropped fund's performance (Elton et al., 2007). A second study on the hiring and firing of fund managers by 3,400 plan sponsors found that plan sponsors are very attracted to funds with above average returns, and frequently hire their managers to replace existing underperforming fund managers. However, this performance-chasing strategy is futile in the long run. The authors drew the following conclusion: "If the plan sponsors had stayed with fired investment managers, their excess returns would be no different from those delivered by newly hired managers" (Goyal and Wahal, 2008). Plan sponsors might therefore want to follow the advice of Bob Pozen, chairman emeritus of MFS Investment Management, and evaluate their fund managers' performance after three years, not yearly (Pozen, 2009).

The bottom line of these experiments is that the time horizon over which performance information is presented to plan participants can have a significant and unintended deleterious influence on their investment behavior. Vendors' current practice of routinely presenting short-term performance information before presenting any longer-term information appears to be causing plan participants to take a short-term view in their investment decisions. Specifically, it tends to cause them to be myopic investors.

Being a myopic investor is as unwise in a bull market as it is in a bear market. We've seen that the myopic response to losses can make participants overly conservative for the long term. Equally, in a rising market myopic investors might invest more aggressively than they probably should in the long term. Both of

these myopic responses to different market conditions are espe
cially important when new hires make investment elections.
The reason is that once this initial allocation has been selected,
most people do not change their contribution allocation for the
lifetime of the account (Samuelson and Zeckhauser, 1988).
Because of inertia, new hires who enroll in the midst of a bear
market might be stuck with an overly conservative portfolio.
Equally, those who enroll in the midst of a bull market might be
stuck with an overly aggressive portfolio.

Myopic investors also tend not to sleep well. Consider this.
The more often an investor checks on his or her portfolio, the
greater the likelihood of seeing a loss at any particular time,
even in a rising market. As we know, experiencing a loss causes
anxiety. Over time, the myopic investor is therefore likely to be
both more conservative or more aggressive in his or her investment strategy than the investor who takes a long-term view, and
also to suffer more sleepless nights over the periodic losses he or
she inevitably observes (Kahneman, Wakker, and Sarin, 1997).
We are therefore looking for a way to help plan participants to
be long-term investors, who will have a more consistent long-
term investment strategy and who will lose less sleep over losses
because they don't see them as frequently.

THE LIFETIME STATEMENT

Plan sponsors are required by law to inform plan participants of
the status of their account each quarter, as noted earlier. But
there is no requirement that the quarterly performance figure
be the most prominent piece of information in the statement.
Plan sponsors have some freedom over the order in which
required information is presented, but, as we saw, most quarterly
statements present quarterly performance prominently on page
one. We have also noted that about a quarter of plan participants

don't read quarterly statements at all and almost three-quarters of those who do spend less than three minutes reading them (Koster, 2009). For those who do read quarterly statements, the question is, What should the statements' objective be, and how best can they achieve it?

As the above research has shown, the quarterly statement should *not* focus plan participants' attention on the short term, because that creates the mind-set of the myopic investor. Instead, it should focus plan participants' attention on the long term, because that is the journey they are on. The first step in transforming the goal and impact of the quarterly statement, then, is to change its name. We propose calling it the "Lifetime Statement," which immediately conveys a different impression about the relevant time horizon. The second step is to select what information should be included and the order in which it should be presented.

We believe that 90 percent of the impact of the quarterly statement on plan participants' perceptions comes from what is on page one (Payne, 2011). If we want plan participants to adopt a long-term perspective in their investment behavior, we can therefore change the quarterly statement in a simple, powerful way: have the lifetime performance of the account be the only performance information displayed on page one, and ensure that it is prominently placed. Given that most plan participants pay only cursory attention to the statement, for the most part probably not getting past the first page, the account's long-term performance information will be what catches most people's attention. This would reverse the unintended consequence of the quarterly statement as currently presented, and help encourage participants to be long-term, rather than myopic, investors.

The remainder of the Lifetime Statement could look much like current quarterly statements, giving details of asset allocation, performance of individual investment funds, future contribution allocation, and so on. Page three, not far into the report, would present the account's overall performance, broken down into three time lines: long-term performance, last twelve months, and quarterly, in that order.

The transformation of the quarterly statement to the Lifetime Statement, as described, is a good start to helping plan participants avoid becoming myopic investors. A second unintended consequence of the quarterly statement is what might be called the "illusion of wealth." Plan sponsors are required to include a figure for the account's balance to date. For someone who has been contributing and investing for a decade or two, this balance can begin to look quite impressive, deceptively so. A balance of $250,000 can look like a lot of money, especially for someone earning, say, $50,000 a year, surely enough to retire on comfortably? Far from it, as we will see in the next chapter. A second change in the quarterly (now Lifetime) statement—presenting projected monthly retirement income—is described in that chapter. It further addresses myopic loss aversion and the illusion of wealth just mentioned.

COUNTERARGUMENTS

I like the idea, but I'm not sure if my record keeper will be able to implement this.

> The changes we are suggesting are not arduous, and most record keepers should be able to implement them. If your record keeper fails to do so, keep this ability and other behavioral finance capabilities in mind when you hire a new record keeper.

I can see why the short investment horizon is not appropriate for younger plan participants, but what about those

somewhat older people, in their fifties, for example? Shouldn't they be interested in short-term performance?

An employee in his or her mid-fifties still has, on average, three decades of life ahead, so a long time horizon is therefore still appropriate. These people will want to know what their retirement accounts will buy them in retirement, increasingly so as they get closer to that day, and we deal with this in the following chapter.

Because of inertia, many plan participants won't shift their investment strategy in response to short-term movements of the markets, so perhaps this is not so big a problem?

The first part of what you say is correct, but there are two issues here: investment attitudes and well-being. Retirement accounts' Lifetime Statements will help those participants who might otherwise be tempted to act as myopic investors. But taking the long view will also help those who won't necessarily change how they invest but nevertheless worry when they see short-term losses, because of myopic loss aversion. It will help them sleep better.

BEHAVIORAL FINANCE ACTIONS

▶**Action 1:** Change the title of the quarterly statement to Lifetime Statement.

▶**Action 2:** Have the account's lifetime performance information displayed prominently on page one. (Rather than seeing a Lifetime Statement, of course, new hires would best view a plan's long-term performance when they enroll.)

▶**Action 3:** Display long-term, twelve-month, and quarterly performance information, in that order, in the body of the statement, perhaps on page three. (For optimum behavioral health, the Lifetime Statement will include recommendations from Chapter 9.)

REFERENCES

Benartzi, Shlomo, and Richard H. Thaler. 1995. "Myopic Loss Aversion and the Equity Premium Puzzle." *The Quarterly Journal of Economics* 110, no. 1: 73–92.

———. 1999. "Risk Aversion or Myopia? Choices in Repeated Gambles and Retirement Investments." *Management Science* 45, no. 3: 364–81.

Elton, Edwin J., Martin J. Gruber, and Christopher R. Blake. 2007. "Participant Reaction and the Performance of Funds Offered by 401(k) Plans." *Journal of Financial Intermediation* 16, no. 2: 240–71.

Gneezy, Uri, and Jan Potters. 1997. "An Experiment on Risk Taking and Evaluation Periods." *The Quarterly Journal of Economics* 112, no, 2: 631–45.

Gneezy, Uri, Arie Kapteyn, and Jan Potters. 2003. "Evaluation Periods and Asset Prices in a Market Experiment." *The Journal of Finance* 57, no. 2: 821–37.

Goyal, Amit, and Sunil Wahal. 2008. "The Selection and Termination of Investment Management Firms by Plan Sponsors." *Journal of Finance* 63, no. 4: 1805–47.

Haigh, Michael S., and John A. List. 2005. "Do Professional Traders Exhibit Myopic Loss Aversion?" *The Journal of Finance* 60, no. 1: 523–34.

Kahneman, Daniel, Peter P. Wakker, and Rakesh Sarin. 1997. "Back to Bentham? Explorations of Experienced Utility." *The Quarterly Journal of Economics* 112: 375–405.

Koster, Kathleen. 2009. "Trying to Avoid Bad News and Confusion, Many Participants Leave 401(k) Statement Unopened." *Employee Benefit News* (April 15).

List, John A. 2004. "Neoclassical Theory versus Prospect Theory: Evidence from the Marketplace." *Econometrica* 72: 615–25.

Payne, John. 2011. Personal communication.

Pozen, Bob. 2009. "Can We Break the Tyranny of Quarterly Results?" HBR Blog Network. http://blogs.hbr.org/hbr/restoring-american-competitiveness/2009/10/can-we-break-the-tyranny-of-qu.html.

Samuelson, William, and Richard J. Zeckhauser. 1988. "Status Quo Bias in Decision Making." *Journal of Risk and Uncertainty* 1: 7–59.

Thaler, Richard H., Amos Tversky, Daniel Kahneman, and Alan Schwartz. 1997. "The Effect of Myopia and Loss Aversion on Risk Taking: An Experimental Test." *Quarterly Journal of Economics* 112, no. 2: 647–61.

CHAPTER 9

TANGIBLE ACCOUNT STATEMENT

PREVIEW

In order to save adequately for retirement, plan participants need to know whether or not their current saving and investing behavior will deliver a comfortable retirement. For most participants, the traditional quarterly statement isn't helpful, and may indeed lull some into a false sense of security, because the statement includes their account balance, often on page one. Many people find it difficult to comprehend amounts of money, such as a 401(k) account balance, that are significantly larger than amounts they deal with in daily life. This can lead to the "illusion of wealth," wherein moderately large sums of money can loom erroneously larger in people's minds.

In the current context, the illusion of wealth can lead an individual to see a figure of, say, $100,000 displayed on his or her account's quarterly statement, and believe he or she no longer needs to save. In fact, a retiree might need $1 million in his or her account to provide a sustainable yearly income of roughly $40,000 to $50,000. Most people are not on target to achieve this modest goal. People clearly need help in knowing whether their saving and investment decisions are leading to a comfortable retirement future.

We propose to change the information architecture so as to include the *projected monthly income at retirement*, tailored to each individual's saving and investment decisions, in the quarterly statement. We call this the Tangible Account Statement. This simple Behavioral Time Machine tool provides participants with a clear picture of their financial future in a frame that is easy to understand and powerful. It is easy to understand because monthly income is a figure with which everyone is familiar. It is powerful precisely because it is so intuitively easy to grasp. It has, again, what psychologists call affective ease, which means that the information content of the numbers presented is readily understood and pertinent to the matter at hand.

Short-term fluctuations in the markets would have a minimal effect on projected monthly income at retirement, especially for younger participants. By focusing on the projected monthly income at retirement, the Tangible Account Statement therefore also minimizes loss aversion when markets go down in the short term, as they inevitably do, even in rising markets. Plan sponsors and advisers who adopt the Tangible Account Statement are being good information architects, working in employees' best interests.

CHALLENGE: THE ILLUSION OF WEALTH

I had the opportunity some years ago to monitor a major plan provider's customer service line. I recall an exchange between a representative and a woman in her mid-forties, whom we will call Rose (for "rose-colored glasses"). Rose said, "I'd like to stop saving." As he had been trained to do, the rep replied, "Oh, and why is that?" Rose was very clear about her reasons: "Because I have already saved enough money for my retirement." The rep asked Rose how much she had saved. "A little more than $100,000," Rose responded, "that's a lot of money." The rep agreed with her, saying, "Yes, it is a lot of money." The exchange ended with the rep agreeing with Rose that it was just fine if she stopped saving.

I recall the exchange so vividly because it was such a stark demonstration of what people struggle with around the illusion of wealth. I am sure that to Rose, $100,000 was indeed a lot of money, more than she could easily imagine. But from the perspective of saving for retirement, it is woefully inadequate. Every financial professional knows this all too well.

How can Rose or any other average person evaluate what $100,000 in a retirement account implies in terms of future lifestyle? This is definitely a challenging situation. We have seen repeatedly in previous chapters that people often turn to heuristics, or rules of thumb, when faced with challenging situations. A good example we saw in the Introduction was the choice to divide savings equally among a small menu of funds in a retirement account, rather than sit down and calculate what the optimal allocation would be, given the expected returns of the different options. In the current context, Rose (and most of the rest of us) would turn to what psychologist Paul Slovic has called the "affect heuristic." This refers to the very rapid, intuitive judgments people come to when faced with a new situation or new information. It has to do with how we *feel* and the impact of that feeling on our subsequent judgment.

We meet our new primary care physician, and immediately *feel* we can trust him. Or we go into a new restaurant, and immediately *feel* suspicious about the culinary experience we are about to embark on. These judgments of "this is good" or "this is bad" come quickly and automatically, and we might rationalize them later. Consider the following examples, from Slovic et al., 2007:

1. Why do movies have background music? After all, can't we understand the events we are watching and the dialogue we are hearing without music?

   Answer: Music conveys affect and thus enhances meaning even for common human interactions and events.

2. Why are all the models in the mail-order catalog smiling?

   Answer: To link positive affect to the clothing they are selling.

3. Why do packages of food products carry all those little blurbs such as "new," "natural," or "improved"?

   Answer: These are "affective tags" that enhance the attractiveness of the product and increase the likelihood that it will be purchased.

Slovic et al. also peel back a layer of deliberate artifice in the entertainment business, where movie stars are careful to ensure their names do not provoke a negative response in adoring audiences. "One wonders whether the careers of John Denver, Sandra

Dee, and Judy Garland would have been as successful had they performed under their real names—Henry Deutschendorf, Alexandra Zuck, and Frances Gumm," they ask.

The importance of feeling—of affect—in judgment and decision making is now widely recognized, and it relates to the fact that we all effectively have two minds: the quick, intuitive mind and the slower, reflective mind (Stanovich and West, 2000; Kahneman, 2011). It is the intuitive mind at work with the affect heuristic, making that snap judgment based on inchoate feeling. People are often correct with their first impressions, of course. Intuition can be a powerful cognitive force. But sometimes those feelings can lead us astray. Large numbers that are not part of our daily experience—the apparently princely sum of $100,000 that Rose finds so alluring, for example—can readily lead to erroneous judgments.

Rose had an immediate and strong impression of what $100,000 meant in relation to her retirement needs, but she was wrong. She was wrong because $100,000 doesn't have what psychologist John Payne calls "affective ease," a principle that builds on, among other things, the affect heuristic. We met this phrase in the Introduction, when we saw that informing customers at a fast-food restaurant that a double cheeseburger and large fries would deliver a massive 930 calories failed to make people think twice about the indulgence, because most people are unaware that 930 calories is virtually half the recommended daily intake. In the same way, telling Rose that her retirement account boasts a balance of $100,000 lacks affective ease. Neither Rose nor any average plan participant can look at that number and immediately know whether or not it is enough to provide for a comfortable retirement.

No doubt Rose would have been shocked to discover that what she thought were adequate savings translates to a monthly income at retirement of just $333, using the 4 percent rule that's common in the industry to convert wealth to annual income, and then dividing the annual income of $4,000 by twelve months. Most people would be shocked. An easy rule of thumb for translating retirement wealth into monthly income is to divide by 300, for which most people would require a calculator, of course. (This is arrived at by multiplying first by 4 percent or dividing by twenty-five, to get annual income, and again by twelve to arrive at monthly income.) By this calculation, retirement wealth of $1 million would generate a monthly income of $3,333, which is actually less than the average 401(k) plan participant earns at the age of about forty. The point here is that most people's emotional response to the word "millionaire" would be, "That guy's rich." They don't identify with being rich, therefore they don't consider a target of $1 million in their retirement account to be relevant to them. It is simply not intuitive to people whose business is not finance that a million dollars in retirement wealth is rather modest, and often necessary.

To put this in perspective, let us look at the account balances of average plan participants. Figures vary somewhat among different sources, but even the most bullish numbers are modest by any measure. For instance, according to EBRI the average account balance in 2010 for sixty-five-year-olds with more than thirty years of tenure is $192,032 (EBRI, 2011). At the same time, 72 percent of participants are not on target to replace 70 percent of their pre-retirement income (Financial Engines, 2010). These are sobering numbers. Most people clearly need help figuring out if they are on track for a comfortable retirement, and then in taking appropriate action if they are not.

SOLUTION: PROVIDE PROJECTED
MONTHLY RETIREMENT INCOME

The behavioral solution to the above challenge is to change the information architecture so as to provide plan participants with a number that has great affective ease in letting them see immediately if they are saving and investing adequately: projected monthly income at retirement. Monthly income and monthly bills—utilities, rent, and so on—are the basic, everyday realities of everyone's financial world. No need for calculation, no need to try to bring to mind a measure that is new and foreign, no need to struggle with the siren temptations of seemingly large pools of wealth. Projected monthly income (in today's dollars) is as familiar a measure of future financial adequacy as can be imagined.

Consider Rose, whom we imagine to be currently earning $5,000 a month. Her Tangible Account Statement would tell her that if she did indeed stop saving in her mid-forties, as she wanted to, with $100,000 in her account, her projected monthly income (in today's dollars) at retirement would be $333 if the account just kept up with inflation, or alternatively, about double, say $666, if the account outpaced inflation by about 4 percent per year. Rose is probably expecting to receive about $1,500 a month in Social Security, which gives her a total monthly income of just $2,166 at retirement. Rose would be able to see right away that not saving is a very bad idea, and that she needs to start saving more, *now*. The same lesson applies to participants who, unlike Rose, are making contributions to their account and whose projected income (plus Social Security) nevertheless falls well short of their current pay or their aspiration level. Do something about it, *now*.

The third chapter in each of the previous two sections—"The Face Tool" and "The Imagine Exercise"—were each under the umbrella term Behavioral Time Machine. The Face Tool helps people identify with their future selves, and the Imagine Exercise makes their future lifestyles tangible. These behavioral solutions help people become more willing to join a retirement savings program and encourage them to save sufficiently. The behavioral solution in the present chapter—the projected monthly retirement income displayed prominently on the quarterly statement—is also a Behavioral Time Machine tool, the Tangible Account Statement. The goal of the Tangible Account Statement is to enable participants to see clearly where they will be in terms of savings *in the future*, specifically, at the point of retirement. The Tangible Account Statement makes people's financial future very real *in the present*.

Arriving at a figure for monthly income is a two-step process, the first of which is calculating estimated wealth at retirement. There is no magic to this, of course; it is simply a matter of making prudent assumptions about returns on the investments chosen by the individual, projected saving behavior, and inflation. The second step is converting projected wealth to projected income, which adds to the affective ease of that figure. Quarterly statements are required by law to include the account's current balance. There is no such provision for projected wealth at retirement or projected monthly income at retirement. Including such numbers would therefore be innovative for most accounts. In this respect, the current chapter distinguishes itself from Chapter 8, which changed the manner in which legally required information (current balance account) is presented on the quarterly statement. The Tangible Account Statement offers important and helpful information that is not at present legally required.*

---

* The U.S. Departments of Labor and Treasury held joint administrative hearings in 2010 during which including such projections on participant benefit statements was discussed, but these agencies have not yet promulgated regulations in this area.

Providing projected monthly income at retirement on the quarterly statement has benefits beyond helping participants readily see whether they are saving and investing adequately. It would also have the benefit of buffering the reaction to short-term volatility in the markets, as such fluctuations would have limited impact on future total accumulation. This is especially true for younger participants. Providing a figure for projected monthly income would therefore be another tool for dealing with potential myopic loss aversion.

The notion of providing workers with projected monthly income at retirement based on current saving behavior has recently become something of a "hot" topic in the industry. For instance, a bill was introduced into the U.S. Congress in 2009, the Lifetime Income Disclosure Act. This would require plan providers to give participants a figure once a year for estimated lifetime income stream, based on current savings. The bill is, however, currently stalled. At the same time, several plan providers have voluntarily begun providing this information, including TIAA-CREF and Vanguard. An individual's Social Security statement also does this.

These actions were taken with the conviction (but with no direct evidence) that providing projected monthly income would boost both plan participation and rate of saving. No one has directly studied the impact of providing this information on these retirement decisions. There are, however, two lines of evidence that support the suggestion that providing such a behavioral solution (by changing the information architecture) would produce the desired outcomes: first, preliminary experimental studies; and, second, a survey of plan participants' preferences.

Preliminary Experimental Studies

Richard Thaler and I started to think about the impact of projected income estimates on participants' retirement planning behavior more than a decade ago (Benartzi and Thaler, 1999). At the time our focus was on the impact of projected annual income on asset allocation. Recall that in the previous chapter we showed that when subjects saw long-term performance information for stocks and bonds, they allocated significantly more savings to stocks than subjects who saw short-term performance data. The same was true for another group of subjects who saw data on projected income. They also invested more in stocks. More recently Gopi Shah Goda and two colleagues did a large study that attempted to explore the effect of projected income disclosures on saving behavior (Goda et al., 2011).

The study population was nearly 17,000 employees at the University of Minnesota, in October 2010 and May 2011. Goda and her colleagues mailed four-page brochures to the subjects, some of whom were informed of the increase in projected wealth accumulation at retirement that would result from a hypothetical increase in saving rate. Subjects in the second study group were given the same information, plus the increase in projected monthly income. The impact on plan participation was the same in both groups, an increase of around 29 percent. But those who saw an increase in projected monthly income boosted their current saving rate by some 8 percent (or 0.25 percent of salary) compared with those who saw only the increase in accumulation.

While this pioneering research is a start in addressing the key question, it falls short of testing the impact of projected monthly income per se. Most significantly, by presenting information on *changes* in projected income rather than absolute *levels* of future income, there is far less affective ease in the numbers. When people see numbers for the level of projected monthly income, they know immediately what they are looking at, and can make appropriate decisions. Numbers for *changes* in projected monthly income are effectively one step removed from meaningful information.

A Survey of Participants

A recent survey by the American Council of Life Insurers suggests that many workers would welcome projected monthly income estimates as a way to prod them to boost their saving rate (ACLI, 2010). Seven hundred and fifty workers between the ages of forty-five and sixty-five were asked the following question:

> "How valuable would it be to have your employer show you an illustration of how much monthly income you could get, guaranteed for life, starting at age 65, based on the current value of your retirement plan account?"

More than half, 52 percent, said it would be "very valuable" and another 39 percent said it would be "somewhat valuable," giving a total of 91 percent who saw at least some value in this disclosure. Only 2 percent suggested it would be "not at all valuable."

At the same time, 61 percent of subjects said they would begin to save more, if the projected income showed they weren't saving enough; 32 percent said they would now start to monitor their savings in case an increase might be necessary in the future; and an equal percentage said they would change how they allocated their assets. Finally, 85 percent of subjects said they would like to have this information, either in their quarterly statements or on a secure Web site hosted either by their employer or plan provider.

MAKING IT EASY TO TAKE ACTION

We therefore believe that the Behavioral Time Machine tool we are proposing—the projected monthly income at retirement—gives plan participants a simple and easily understood measure of whether or not they are saving enough for retirement. We strongly recommend that the information architecture be changed so that projected income at retirement is displayed prominently on the first page of the quarterly issued Tangible Account Statement. The Lifetime Income Disclosure Act provides for that information only once a year, but we believe its message is more effective if it is presented with every statement.

This is the first provision of the Tangible Account Statement. Of equal importance is easing the path to taking necessary actions. The statement should therefore also prominently display a simple but important question: "Are you satisfied with your projected monthly income?" This question should appear directly underneath the projected monthly income. It should be immediately followed by another statement: "If you answered 'No,' here are some actions to take." This could include checking a box to join an automatic savings escalator program, such as SMarT, or ensuring that the account assets are invested prudently. Whatever the action is, the important thing is that it be obvious and easy.

This second provision of the Tangible Account Statement relates to a lesson learned in the Introduction, and repeated several times in earlier chapters, namely, that providing information to participants is, by itself, insufficient to change people's behavior, no matter how pertinent the information is. We saw in the Introduction that 100 percent of non-participating employees who attended a financial education program declared their intention to join, as a result of what they had heard. But three months later, only 14 percent had acted on their good intentions (Choi et al., 2006). Inertia and procrastination are tough obstacles to overcome, and the great majority of people fail to do anything, even when they know it is the right thing to do, and even when they say that they intend to act. Information is made vastly more valuable if it is accompanied by the means to take action, *right now.*

This brings to mind my own recent experience with quarterly statements. For the past several quarters the loudest and clearest message I was getting, right there on page one, was that I have been losing money pretty much every quarter. Then the statement asked me to take action. What was that action? That I should check a box so that future statements would be delivered electronically—which would, of course, save my record keeper money. Now, I am all for cutting down fewer trees, and protecting the environment. But I do think that record keepers should be doing more than prompting plan participants to save trees. They should be making it easier for plan participants to take actions that improve their retirement outcomes. The Tangible Account Statement does just that.

COUNTERARGUMENTS

My plan provider is unable to customize account statements in the way that you are proposing.

> You are by now familiar with this particular argument about BeFi-challenged plan providers. And the response is as it always is: you will serve the best interests of your employees by finding a plan provider who is BeFi-capable.

If the assumptions are off and my participants' monthly income is below what was projected in their statements, am I liable? Do I have more fiduciary risk if the assumptions don't hold true?

> The U.S. Department of Labor, which has jurisdiction over the fiduciary provisions of federal pension law, issued guidance in 1996 designed to facilitate the provision of investment education materials to participants. Under this widely used guide, general information and tools designed

to help participants make investment decisions, even including individualized model asset allocation portfolios, are deemed not to constitute fiduciary advice. Properly constructed retirement income projections, using prudent assumptions and providing appropriate disclosures and warnings that outcomes cannot be guaranteed, are likely to qualify as non-fiduciary educational materials under this DOL guidance.* While it is true that no one (not even your lawyer) can assure you that you won't be sued because participants using educational materials did not achieve their desired retirement outcomes, and while the authors of this book cannot provide legal advice, it is worth noting that some very large financial-services providers are already providing such projections to many plans and their participants.

Would it be a good idea to include current monthly income on Tangible Account Statements, to give participants a reference point for their adequacy of saving?

Yes, in principle, it would. But in practice it is a little more complicated. When participants are judging the adequacy of their saving and investing behavior, given their projected monthly income on the Tangible Account Statement, they need to take into account several factors. One is monthly Social Security payments, while another may be income from other sources, such as a defined-benefit retirement plan. Displaying current monthly income on the Tangible Account Statement alongside projected monthly income without these other factors might be discouraging, if the

---

* See 29 CFR § 2509.96-1. Note that determinations about any specific plan or program must be based on the particular facts and circumstances.

disparity between them is substantial. In cases such as these, participants might decide the goal is unattainable, and give up trying. Figuring out how best to achieve the goal behind this line of thinking might be part of creating the next generation of quarterly statements.

BEHAVIORAL FINANCE ACTIONS

▶**Action 1:** Discuss with your plan provider what is needed to generate projected monthly retirement income for individual participants.

▶**Action 2:** Have your plan provider replace the traditional quarterly statement with a Tangible Account Statement that prominently displays projected monthly income at retirement.

▶**Action 3:** Ensure that the Tangible Account Statement includes a prominently displayed prompt asking participants if they are satisfied with their projected monthly income, and provide easy actions to change saving rate or asset allocation if participants wish to.

REFERENCES

ACLI. 2010. "ACLI Retirement Choices Study."

Benartzi, Shlomo, and Richard H. Thaler. 1999. "Risk Aversion or Myopia? Choices in Repeated Gambles and Retirement Investments." *Management Science* 45, no. 3: 364–81.

Choi, James J., David Laibson, Brigitte C. Madrian, and Andrew Metrick. 2006. "Defined Contribution Pensions: Plan Rules, Participant Decisions, and the Path of Least Resistance." In *Tax Policy and the Economy*, vol. 16, edited by James Poterba. Cambridge: MIT Press.

EBRI. 2011. "Is There a Future for Retirement?" EBRI-ERF Policy Forum #68.

Financial Engines. 2010. "The Financial Engines National 401(k) Evaluation."

Goda, Gopi Shah, Colleen Flaherty Manchester, and Aaron Sojourner. 2011. "What's My Account Really Worth?" Working paper, Rand Corporation, WR-873.

Slovic, Paul, Melissa Finucane, Ellen Peters, and Donald G. MacGregor. 2007. "The Affect Heuristic." *European Journal of Operational Research* 177, no. 3: 1333–52.

Stanovich, Keith E., and Richard F. West. 2000. "Individual Differences in Reasoning: Implications for the Rationality Debate." *Behavioral and Brain Sciences* 23, no. 5: 645–65.

BEHAVIORAL FINANCE IN ACTION

CHAPTER 10

THE PLANSUCCESS
BEHAVIORAL AUDIT

The previous nine chapters described a series of behavioral challenges employers and employees face in making decisions around joining, saving, and investing in 401(k) plans. Inertia, loss aversion, and myopia often prevent people from making good decisions, with the issue of self-control often cropping up, too. We have shown how these challenges can be transformed into behavioral opportunities for creating solutions to those challenges. These behavioral opportunities are, in effect, behavioral finance tools that, collectively, represent a behavioral finance toolbox. Plan sponsors will find these tools very easy to use; and in their turn, the tools offer carefully designed choice and information architectures that make it easy for employees to make good individual decisions around retirement planning. As a result, the plan sponsor will have what we can describe as a behaviorally healthy 401(k) plan.

Behaviorally healthy 401(k) plans should have a high participation rate, adequate savings levels, and prudent portfolio choices. In other words, all the behavioral challenges will have been successfully overcome, and plan participants will have made wise decisions for their retirement future.

While *Save More Tomorrow* puts a heavy emphasis on the new science of behavioral finance, it is more than an academic review of the behavioral challenges around 401(k) plans and the appropriate behavioral solutions. It is an *action* plan, a powerful set of tools with which plan sponsors can boost the behavioral health of their 401(k) plans. The PlanSuccess System is the process we have developed to systematically employ this behavioral finance toolbox. It is a dynamic process with three interconnected components, shown in the diagram below:

———————— How the PlanSuccess System Works ————————

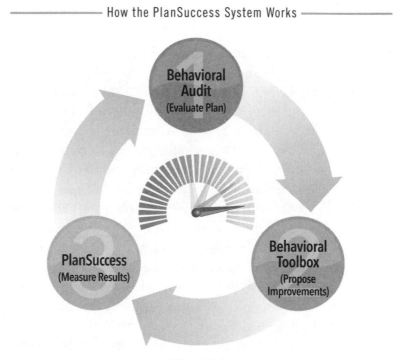

Figure 10–1.

As we've said, Chapters 1 through 9 collectively represent the behavioral finance toolbox, shown bottom-right in the diagram. It's a practical toolbox created from the very latest science of behavioral finance. But even the best toolbox is useless unless it is effectively implemented. After all, how many people go to conferences and workshops, hear new and powerful ideas, then fail to put them into action on Monday morning? Inertia is, as we know, a powerful behavioral challenge that often prevents us from doing what we know we should be doing. This final chapter is designed to overcome the Monday morning inertia factor. It is a practical guide to help plan sponsors and their advisers put the behavioral toolbox to work, boost the behavioral health of their 401(k) plans, and ensure that plans stay healthy. This practical guide is the PlanSuccess Behavioral audit, which is described below. As noted in the introductory chapter, plan sponsors and advisers will also want to conduct a fiduciary audit, to guard against participants paying excessive fees, for example.

The principal thrust of this chapter, then, is the PlanSuccess Behavioral Audit, and the appropriate response to the audit. The PlanSuccess Behavioral Audit evaluates the current behavioral health of a 401(k) plan and indicates which behavioral tools need to be applied, and how to apply them. The third component of the system, PlanSuccess, measures the impact of the behavioral intervention and indicates what further application of behavioral tools should be taken, if any is necessary. Optimally, the process is repeated yearly so as to ensure the continued behavioral health of the plan.

The overall process is as follows:

▶ **Behavioral Audit:** Financial advisers collect data on participation, savings, the makeup of the investment menu, and how plan sponsors administer and construct their plans. All of this would be available from the record keeper, though it could also be collected directly from the plan sponsor. The performance of the plan would be measured against both the 90—10—90 Plan-Success goals and the best behavioral practices.

▶ **Behavioral Toolbox:** Deficiencies in the plan would be addressed by the appropriate behavioral finance solutions described in the body of the book. A low participation rate might call for a change from Auto-Grounded to Auto-Takeoff, for instance. A low saving rate might call for the implementation of automatic enrollment into a savings escalator, such as Save More Tomorrow™, or Auto-Climb. Auto-Smooth might be necessary to help the majority of participants have a well-diversified portfolio. And so on.

▶ **PlanSuccess:** The impact of the intervention would be measured by a re-application of the PlanSuccess Behavioral Audit one year later, and at repeated intervals in the future.

The PlanSuccess Behavioral Audit is based on the principle of the checklist, a device that Duke University psychologist John Payne describes as "the most powerful decision tool ever invented" (Payne, 2011). Checklists in the workplace are a formalized version of everyday household "to do" lists. They are simple but highly effective memory aids for people who have many demands on their attention. Probably the most well-known professional checklist is the aviation safety checklist, the origin of which is quite instructive and is described in a recent book by Atul Gawande (Gawande, 2011).

On October 30, 1935, the U.S. Army Air Corps held a flight competition for the next-generation long-range bomber. Boeing's entry, the Model 299, was the odds-on favorite to win over the planes designed by Martin and Douglas. It could carry more bombs and fly faster and further than the competition; it had been dubbed the "Flying Fortress." The outcome of the competition that day was therefore assumed to be a foregone conclusion, and the army planned to order at least sixty-five Model 299s. The huge plane roared down the runway, took off smoothly, and rapidly reached three hundred feet, at which point it stalled, turned on one wing, and crashed in a ball of fire, killing two of the five-member crew, including Boeing's chief test pilot, Leslie Tower. Not the kind of performance likely to impress prospective customers. The Army Air Corps named Douglas's smaller design the winner of the day, and Boeing nearly went bankrupt.

An investigation of the crash concluded it had been the result of pilot error. The plane was much more complex than anything that had previously taken to the skies. It required the pilot to, among other tasks, pay attention to four engines, a retractable landing gear, new wing flaps, and many more new features. As one newspaper put it, the Flying Fortress was "too much airplane for one man to fly." In this newly demanding technical environment, the pilot had forgotten to disengage the "gust lock," a device that held the plane's moveable control surfaces in place while parked on the ground. The plane was therefore not flyable once it took off, and the result was disaster.

Despite this initial debacle, a small group of test pilots were unwilling to give up on the giant aircraft, and got together to figure out what needed to be done so that it could be flown safely. The first thing they decided was that having pilots undergo extra training wasn't the answer. After all, the pilot on the day of the crash had been the Air Corps' chief of testing. No pilot was more skilled or experienced than he was. Instead, they hit on the idea of a checklist, actually several: pre-flight, in-flight, and a checklist for landing. Each was simple, and short enough to fit on an index card. Each was a step-by-step list of necessary actions required for safe takeoff, flight, and landing. It wasn't rocket science, just lists of actions that trained pilots knew about but which, taken together, were too much for one person's memory to reliably bring to mind every time. The pilot's omission that doomed the plane on that late October day was a simple maneuver that just didn't come to his mind in the blizzard of other technical demands. Had there been a checklist, the gust lock would have been released, and all would have been well.

Going through a pre-flight checklist was exactly what Charles Lindbergh had done eight years earlier when he set off from Roosevelt Field on Long Island to fly solo and nonstop across the Atlantic. He kept a comprehensive checklist of all his equipment and flying procedures, and constantly checked and rechecked them to make sure everything was right before, during, and after each flight. But checklists didn't become a routine part of aviation practice until after the experience with Boeing's Flying Fortress. After that disastrous October day, pilots, checklists in hand, went on to fly the plane 1.8 million miles without incident. The Army Air Corps eventually ordered nearly thirteen thousand of the aircraft, and Boeing pulled back from the brink of bankruptcy it faced after that initial failure.

The PlanSuccess Behavioral Audit is designed to do for the Retirement Plane journey what the checklist did for Boeing's Flying Fortress: ensure a safe and secure takeoff and flight, in this case on the challenging journey to a comfortable retirement, every time.

The PlanSuccess System process begins with the Behavioral Audit, two dozen process questions (listed in Appendix 2). This is the PlanSuccess System's checklist. These detailed questions are built around a superstructure of three outcome questions that are tied to the 90—10—90 PlanSuccess goals. The three questions are:

What is the participation rate for your plan?
What is the average employee deferral rate for your plan?
What percentage of plan participants are invested in
    default investment funds?

According to our PlanSuccess goals, a behaviorally healthy retirement plan will have at least 90 percent of employees participating; they will defer at least 10 percent of their pay to their retirement account (plus a generous employer match); and around 90 percent of plan participants will be invested in a one-stop, professionally managed portfolio, such as a target-date fund. The PlanSuccess Behavioral Audit reveals where a retirement plan is falling short of these goals, which leads to suggestions and recommendations for what behavioral finance solutions plan sponsors and their advisers should implement to improve the behavioral health of the plan.

As this book was going to press, several dozen such Behavioral Audits had been carried out, and found that all the plans fell short of the 90—10—90 PlanSuccess goals. Most of the audits were initiated and carried out by Don M. Faller, CFP, and Jamie Hayes, QPFC, partners in FiduciaryFirst, an independent retirement plan advisory firm based in Florida. Don and Jamie have enthusiastically embraced behavioral finance solutions to behavioral challenges that employers and employees face in making retirement plan decisions. "Don and I are passionate about our clients' success," explains Jamie. "As industry leaders and specialists, we have a social responsibility to do what's right for our clients and their employees. [The PlanSuccess Behavioral Audit] allows us to fulfill our passion to improve participant outcomes to get them to retire comfortably" (Hayes, 2011).

By way of illustrating the audit and subsequent recommendation part of the process, we will present here the results of one such audit that Don and Jamie carried out in the summer of 2011. The plan sponsor was Orbitz Worldwide, a leading global online travel company. Barney Harford, CEO of Orbitz, explains his company's decision to undergo the audit in this way:

"Orbitz has an excellent plan that exceeds industry benchmarks. However, we feel as a plan sponsor that we should always strive to do better and set the bar higher. The behavioral finance audit we have gone through offered us new tools to make our plan even more successful and further improve outcomes."

The results of the audit are displayed below, in the same 3 x 3 chapter matrix format that we presented in the Introduction. (Cell 1 of the matrix concerns behavioral challenges and behavioral solutions discussed in Chapter 1, and so on.) In doing this, we have simplified the responses to the many process questions and we present them in a concise way here to highlight the most important points.

──────── Behavioral Audit Fact Finding ────────

	Design Easy Choices to Address Inertia	Manage Losses to Address Loss Aversion	Provide Behavioral Time Machines to Address Myopia
Save	**Chapter 1. Auto-Takeoff:** Auto-takeoff for new employees only, with a default deferral of 3 percent and no "future enrollment."	**Chapter 2. Match Optimizer:** Match dollar-for-dollar up to 3 percent of pay.	**Chapter 3. The Face Tool:** Face Tool not yet available. In development.
Save More	**Chapter 4. Save More Tomorrow 1.0:** Savings escalator offered just for new employees, with a 1 percent annual increment, up to 6 percent of pay.	**Chapter 5. Save More Tomorrow 2.0:** Saving increases take place on anniversary of participant enrollment in the program.	**Chapter 6. The Imagine Exercise:** No tools offered to help employees envision their financial future and related emotions.
Save Smarter	**Chapter 7. Investment Solutions Pyramid:** New employees defaulted to a target-date fund. Order of the 29 total funds offered is random.	**Chapter 8. The Lifetime Statement:** Quarterly statement focuses on short-term performance.	**Chapter 9. Tangible Account Statement:** Projected monthly income at retirement not displayed.

Figure 10–2.

Before we examine the matrix in any detail, here are the results of the three outcomes questions for this plan described earlier, and that are not part of the matrix:

- 87 percent of employees participate in the company's 401(k) plan.
- The average deferral rate is 7.74 percent.
- 42 percent of employees invest in default investment funds.

A quick perusal of the matrix reveals that the plan sponsor is aware of behavioral finance tools to improve employees' decisions around planning for retirement. For instance, the plan includes Auto-Takeoff (cell 1 of the matrix) and automatic enrollment in a savings escalator program (cell 4), both of which are to be applauded. However, the devil is in the details. Take a look at how these two programs have been implemented. Auto-Takeoff applies only to new employees, and leaves non-participating employees Auto-Grounded; and the initial deferral rate is just 3 percent. Similarly, the automatic savings escalator (Auto-Climb) applies only to new employees, with a 1 percent annual increment, up to 6 percent of pay. In their roles as choice and information architects, the plan sponsor in this case has followed the guidelines of the Pension Protection Act of 2006.

But, as we pointed out in Chapter 4, these guidelines explicitly represent minimum targets: a *minimum* initial contribution of 3 percent, and, at the same time, a *minimum* automatic savings increase of 1 percent a year, with a *minimum* target of 6 percent. Plan sponsors are free to choose higher initial deferral rates, a bigger increment, and a higher target savings rate. However, the great majority of plan sponsors appear to view these minimum suggestions as *prescriptions*, and apply them. As a result, because of inertia, participants are likely to stick with the

———————— Behavioral Audit Recommendations ————————

	Design Easy Choices to Address Inertia	Manage Losses to Address Loss Aversion	Provide Behavioral Time Machines to Address Myopia
Save	Chapter 1. Auto-Takeoff: Implement Auto-Takeoff for all employees, double the default deferral rate to 6 percent, and offer "future enrollment	Chapter 2. Match Optimizer: Change match formula to 30 cents on the dollar up to 10 percent of pay.	Chapter 3. The Face Tool: Offer the Face Tool when it becomes available.
Save More	Chapter 4. Save More Tomorrow 1.0: Offer savings escalator to all employees, double annual increase to 2 percent, and raise target saving rate to 10 percent.	Chapter 5. Save More Tomorrow 2.0: Synchronize savings increases with pay increases, or set increase date to January 1.	Chapter 6. The Imagine Exercise: Offer tools to help employees envision their financial future and related emotions.
Save Smarter	Chapter 7. Investment Solutions Pyramid: Default all employees to target date funds. For those participants who elect to choose, position TDFs at the top of the menu. Break the investment menu into, first, target-date funds, second, a manageable set (5 – 9) of core funds, and third, specialty funds.	Chapter 8. The Lifetime Statement: Offer a Lifetime Statement, which emphasizes long-term performance.	Chapter 9. Tangible Account Statement: Display projected monthly income on the quarterly statement.

Figure 10–3.

low deferral rate and will finish up saving less than the PlanSuccess goal of at least 10 percent. Indeed, we see above that the average deferral in the plan is 7.74 percent.

You can see from the other cells in the above matrix that this plan is deficient in other behavioral measures, too, such as not offering tools to help participants envision their financial future (and incorporating related emotions), and a focus on short-term performance. In this respect, this plan is typical of most plans in 2011. These behavioral deficiencies represent opportunities to implement behavioral solutions in the company's plan. The solutions presented to the plan sponsor are shown in the Behavioral Audit recommendations, displayed in the same 3 x 3 chapter matrix form as the Behavioral Audit Recommendations. (See Figure 10-3.)

We won't go through the matrix cell by cell. You can do so at your leisure, and you will find each set of solutions discussed in detail in the respective chapters. Instead, we will look at a few in some detail, pulling out both specific and general points.

Let's consider participation. The participation rate in this plan is already quite healthy, 87 percent. This, of course, is the outcome of implementing Auto-Takeoff, which typically lifts participation rates up to this level. But this company has an opportunity to do even better, first by offering Auto-Takeoff to existing employees, and second, by instituting "future enrollment" (cell 1 in the recommendations matrix). Because of inertia, non-participating employees are likely to stay in the plan once they have been automatically enrolled. And future enrollment is likely to help a significant proportion of those employees who opt out to commit now to joining at some point in the future. By implementing these two behavioral solutions, the plan sponsor might well boost eventual participation close to 100 percent.

At the same time, the Behavioral Audit recommendations include doubling the default saving rate, from 3 to 6 percent (also cell 1). We saw earlier that many employers say they are reluctant to go higher than 3 percent, fearing that participants might find a higher deferral too demanding, and cause more to opt out. However, research shows that the opt-out rate for initial deferrals of 3 and 6 percent is virtually identical. By being bolder and going for the higher deferral rate, plan sponsors will help employees reach the PlanSuccess goal of at least 10 percent saving much more quickly. That general point applies to the specific plan we are discussing.

The plan sponsor automatically enrolls new employees who do not make an affirmative election to join their 401(k) plan in a savings escalator program, which makes it one of the more progressive employers in this realm. (Less than 40 percent of plans with Auto-Takeoff also have automatic enrollment in a savings escalator program, or Auto-Climb: PSCA, 2011.) But once again, offering the program to *all* employees—new and existing—would extend its reach. The plan sponsor could also be a little more progressive, by doubling the annual savings increase to 2 percent a year, thus helping participants more quickly get to the PlanSuccess goal of 10 percent saving rate (cell 4). Boosting the saving rate can be made more palatable by synchronizing the saving increase with pay increases, thus avoiding loss aversion that might be triggered when participants see their paychecks go down a little. And if that's not possible, a saving increase date of January 1 is often acceptable, because of the turning-over-a-new-leaf effect (cell 5).

Another route to achieving the 10 percent goal is to modify the employer match. Currently the match formula is dollar-for-dollar, up to 3 percent of pay. The plan sponsor's cost of this match, therefore, is 3 percent of payroll. But we saw in Chapter 2 that the match cap is like a beacon for those participants who elect a savings rate for themselves, and save at that rate (those who opt out of Auto-Climb). One of the Behavioral Audit recommendations, therefore, is to increase the cap to 10 percent and at the same time reduce the match rate to thirty cents on the dollar (cell 2). Those participants who select the savings rate for themselves are now likely to increase their deferral to 10 percent. And the new match formula would not increase the employer's costs, because it remains at 3 percent of payroll.

Finally, let's look at the investment options the plan sponsor offers participants. Cell 7 of the Behavioral Audit Fact Finding matrix reveals that the plan has a menu of twenty-nine funds, twelve of which are target-date funds (2000 to 2055, in five-year increments) and seventeen core funds. Only new employees are defaulted into a target-date fund. Existing employees therefore face the task of constructing a portfolio by choosing from a lengthy menu of investment options that are not organized in any particular order.

We saw above that the Behavioral Audit recommendations included Auto-Takeoff and Auto-Climb for existing as well as new employees. The same recommendation applies here, too. *All* employees should be defaulted into an appropriate target-date fund, because in most cases this is what a large proportion of workers want. And they are typically not sufficiently knowledgeable to do a good job of selecting a well-diversified portfolio. A small proportion of people—around 10 percent—are likely to opt out, and the following recommendations are for them.

We saw in Chapter 7 that the order in which funds are offered is likely to have a significant influence on which options are chosen: those at the head of the list are likely to be selected preferentially. The Behavioral Audit recommendation, therefore, is to break the menu into three parts for those participants who opt out of the target-date fund that has been selected for them. First, place the target-date funds at the top of the list; second, offer between five and nine core funds; third, finish the menu with specialty funds. This grouping is tailored to the different appetites for involvement in investment decisions among participants. Those with little appetite will find themselves selecting from the top or near-top of the list, while those with the appetite and skill to be more involved investors might include specialty funds in their portfolio.

As is common with virtually all plans that we know of, this one lacks behavioral tools to help employees think more clearly about the future. Present bias is very strong in most of us, and it takes an effort to see ourselves in the future and to take a long-term view of our actions, instead of focusing myopically on the short term. The Behavioral Audit recommendations in cells 6, 8, and 9 provide the needed guidance. The Imagine Exercise, or some other similar process, helps make people's future lifestyle experiences more tangible in the present. At the same time, the Lifetime and Tangible Account Statements put the future financial reality in concrete terms *now* in a way that the traditional quarterly statement does not. Indeed, as we saw in Chapter 8, the traditional quarterly statement has the unintended consequence of turning participants into myopic investors.

So we have here a matrix of recommendations that are tailored to this particular plan sponsor's choice architecture. This focus on the behavioral health of individual plans is a key strength of the PlanSuccess Behavioral Audit. Although many plans will share similar behavioral deficiencies, the audit identifies specific deficiencies, and degrees of deficiency, for each plan under scrutiny. And the Behavioral Audit recommendations are customized to address these deficiencies.

We noted earlier that the plan under scrutiny in this chapter displayed a significant awareness of behavioral finance tools designed to improve retirement plan decisions. But there is room for improvement because of how these tools have been implemented—adopting Auto-Takeoff, but with a low initial deferral rate, and adopting Auto-Climb, but with a low saving increment, for example. This brings us to a second key strength of the PlanSuccess System process: it reveals where *implementation* of behavioral tools is inadequate. And correct implementation of tools—whether you are fixing your lawn mower or fixing the behavioral health of a 401(k) plan—is vital to success. (Auto-

Takeoff with a higher initial deferral rate helps participants save more, as does Auto-Climb with a higher saving increment, and so on.)

This chapter, then, is in part the story of a plan sponsor, Orbitz Worldwide, who set off with good intentions on the path toward a behaviorally healthy 401(k) plan, but still needs to implement additional measures to reach its laudable goal. But the story continues for Orbitz because its CEO, Barney Harford, understood that the plan needed help, embraced the potential of behavioral finance solutions, and was open to the scrutiny of the PlanSuccess Behavioral Audit. Harford can be thought of as a modern-day Charles Lindbergh in a different context, applying a behavioral checklist to his plan to improve outcomes in the Retirement Plane journey. This was in the fall of 2011, so we will have to be patient and wait a year to see how the plan's behavioral health has improved, and which areas need further attention.

Our modern-day Charles Lindbergh need not be alone: every plan sponsor could be helped by the PlanSuccess System to, in Jamie's words, help their employees retire comfortably.

250 SAVE MORE TOMORROW

REFERENCES

Gawande, Atul. 2011. *The Checklist Manifesto: How to Get Things Right.*
  New York: Picador.
Hayes, Jamie. 2011. Personal communication.
PSCA. 2011. "54th Annual Survey."

CONCLUDING REMARKS AND THE WAY FORWARD

I said in the Introduction that in reading *Save More Tomorrow* you were embarking on a journey into the behavioral world of financial decision making. It is in many ways a strange world, where the human factor turns the unexpected into the norm, and where people sometimes behave in apparently very curious ways. You have now come to that journey's end, and together we are ready to reflect on the experience in preparation for the next step: action.

Many of you will have been at least somewhat familiar with some of the ideas around behavioral finance when you first opened this book, others less so. Whatever the case, I am confident that you now look at the world through new eyes, able to see and understand why people often make retirement planning decisions that are simply not in their best interests, those curious behaviors. More important, you are also able to see that the behavioral challenges that cause people to make unwise decisions can be effectively countered by transforming those challenges into opportunities for tailored behavioral solutions. These are the behavioral finance tools described in Chapters 1 through 9.

By embarking on this journey into the behavioral world you have been, and will continue to be, at the cutting edge of your professional worlds. I want to say just three things about where this enterprise has taken us, and where we are going.

First, you have seen that behavioral finance tools work, and often can powerfully improve outcomes. They powerfully improve outcomes because they make it easy for people to get on the right course for joining, saving, and investing in their company's retirement plan. No need to list the examples of improved outcomes here; you have seen the evidence in Chapters 1 through 9. Suffice it to say that by being wise choice architects and wise information architects, plan sponsors and their advisers can dramatically improve their employees' retirement prospects.

Second, we have in place a process, the PlanSuccess System, to implement the behavioral solutions in the behavioral finance toolbox in a systematic way, beginning with the PlanSuccess Behavioral Audit. Like the checklist that ensures a plane's safe journey from takeoff to climbing to cruising to its destination, the PlanSuccess System ensures that the journey of the Retirement Plane is equally safe.

Third, with the widespread implementation of the behavioral finance tools offered in this book, we have an opportunity and an obligation to monitor the outcomes of these innovative interventions and to measure the improvements in participation, saving, and investing behaviors in each case. We have an opportunity to learn from the experience, and, as we learn, further hone the tools for even better outcomes as we go forward. Behavioral finance is still a young science and a young practice. Our collective experience with implementing the tools described in *Save More Tomorrow* will be an important part of its maturation.

Thank you for joining me on the journey into the behavioral world laid out in the pages of this book. It is now time to embark on the journey of improving 401(k) outcomes in the real world—your world—as plan sponsors and financial advisers. It is an ambitious journey, and you are the pioneers embarking on it. And we invite any of you who would like to be involved in future studies to please contact me at the Allianz Center for Behavioral Finance: contactus@allianzbefi.com

Bon Voyage!

APPENDIX 1

Retirement Savings Questionnaire[*]

1. In your opinion, what percentage of employees with access to a 401(k) plan should be enrolled in the plan and saving for retirement?_____%

2. What percentage of salary do you think a typical 401(k) participant should be deferring to reach his or her retirement goals?_____%

3. In a typical plan, what percentage of participants would be better off selecting one-stop portfolio solutions, such as target-date funds or model portfolios, instead of self-constructing their own mix of funds?_____%

---

* Conducted with two groups. The first was the group of nineteen attendees of the Allianz Global Investors Retirement Summit, held in Dallas in May 2011. The second group was 115 attendees at the Center for Due Diligence Advisor Conference in Chicago, October 2011.

APPENDIX 2

PlanSuccess Behavioral Audit Questions

These questions address two kinds of issues: outcomes and processes. Questions A, B, and C are about outcomes, specifically the rate of plan participation, savings rate, and percentage in default investment funds. The numbered questions focus on processes, that is, steps that can be taken to influence outcomes. The numbers indicate the appropriate chapter.

SECTION 1: SAVE

CHAPTERS 1–3

A: What is the participation rate for your plan?

1a: Does your plan use auto-enrollment for *new employees*?

1b: Does your plan use auto-enrollment for *existing employees*?

1c: What is the initial deferral rate for auto-enrolled participants?

1d: Does your plan offer *easy-enrollment*?

1e: Does your plan offer *active-enrollment*?

1f: Does your plan offer a *future-enrollment* option when an employee decides not to participate in the plan?

2: What is the maximum percentage of pay that the employer will match? (For example, if the employer matches fifty cents on the dollar for up to 6% of pay, the answer here would be 6% not 3%.)

3 Coming Soon: The Face Tool

We're working on a new solution designed to help motivate employees to save more for retirement. The "Face Tool" will use age-progression technology to show workers a vivid image of their future selves. Studies have shown this kind of exercise can result in participants saving significantly more for retirement.

We'll keep you posted as this tool becomes available. Meanwhile, you can read more about this and other behavioral finance solutions in this book and in the *New York Times* article, "Looking Ahead to the Spend Down Years." [link to article is http://www.nytimes.com/2010/09/16/business/retirementspecial/16SAVE.html?pagewanted=all]

SECTION 2: SAVE MORE

CHAPTERS 4–6

B: What's the average employee deferral rate for your plan?

4a: Does your plan use a savings escalator program of deferrals for *new employees*?

4b: Does your plan use a savings escalator program of deferrals for *existing employees*?

4c: If your plan already uses a savings escalator program, what is the percentage by which employee contribution rates are increased annually?

4d: At what percentage of salary is the savings escalator capped?

5a: Does your plan implement the savings escalator increase to coincide with salary increases?

5b: If the answer to 5a is "No," when do savings escalator increases occur?

> *Choose one:*
>
> Every January, as designated by the employer
>
> Other (please specify)

6: People have a strong tendency to focus on the short term and often have difficulty thinking concretely about the future. Do you offer specific tools to participants to help them envision their own retirements?

SECTION 3: SAVE SMARTER

CHAPTERS 7–9

C: What percentage of plan participants are invested in default investment funds?

7a: Does your plan offer a default investment choice for new employees?

Choose one:

Yes—Target-date fund

Yes—Target-risk fund

Yes—Balanced fund

Yes—Third-party managed accounts

Yes—Other: Please specify (for example, cash or stable value) _____

No—No default offered

7b: Does your plan offer a default investment choice for existing employees?

Choose one:

Yes—Target-date fund

Yes—Target-risk fund

Yes—Balanced fund

Yes—Third-party managed accounts

Yes—Other: Please specify (for example, cash or stable value) _____

No—No default offered

7c: How is your plan's fund menu typically presented to participants?

Choose one:

a) According to risk, with safest funds listed first

b) Starting with funds that are appropriate for the widest range of investors (such as target-date funds)

c) In alphabetical order

d) Other: Please specify_____

7d: How many investment options does your plan offer in the following categories?

a) One-stop portfolio solutions

b) Core

c) Specialty

7e: One strategy used to group funds is to target one-stop funds for most employees, core funds for a smaller base of employees who are more self-directed, and specialty funds for expert investors. Do you use this system of grouping funds in your plan?

7f: What percentage of plan assets is in company stock?

8: On account statements, do you present long-term performance information before you present quarterly performance information?

9: Do account statements show participants their projected income at retirement, given their current savings trajectory?

INDEX

About the Allianz Global Investors Center for Behavioral Finance

The Allianz Global Investors Center for Behavioral Finance was founded in 2010 with the goal of empowering people to make better financial decisions and achieve better financial outcomes. To accomplish this, the Center transforms academic research into actionable ideas and practical tools for financial advisors and plan sponsors to use with their clients and employees.

The Center for Behavioral Finance carries on the Allianz Global Investors commitment to innovative thinking. The firm has long been dedicated to helping its clients make better decisions by offering them unique insights into the economy and the financial markets. Helping them better understand and address the human element supplies the missing piece. The Center also seeks to stimulate dialog among business, government and academic leaders on financial issues of importance to the United States and the world at large.

For more information, or to access our publications and videos, visit befi.allianzgi.com, or email contactus@allianzbefi.com.